PIAZZAS

POPES

& PASTA

NOTES FROM A ROME SOJOURN

LUANNE D. ZURLO

Available from:
Marian Helpers Center
Stockbridge, MA 01263

Prayerline: 1-800-804-3823
Orderline: 1-800-462-7426

Websites: thedivinemercy.org
marian.org

Publication Date:
August 12, 2018

Imprimi Potest:
Very Rev. Kazimierz Chwalek, MIC
Provincial Superior
The Blessed Virgin Mary, Mother of Mercy Province
March 17, 2018

Nihil Obstat:
Dr. Robert A. Stackpole, STD
Censor Deputatus
March 17, 2017

ISBN: 978-1-59614-433-0

Cover and page design: Curtis Bohner

Printed in the United States of America

MARIAN PRESS
STOCKBRIDGE   MA 01263

For my parents, Charlotte and Eugene Zurlo,
who paved my road to Rome

Contents

Foreword

I wrote *Fifteen Feet from the Pope* during the fall and winter of 2013–14, while on a sabbatical in Rome. A friend's request to write about my experiences and impressions served as the initial inspiration. I dutifully complied and wrote a series of long emails which I referred to as 'dispatches.' I unexpectedly found great pleasure in writing these 'dispatches' and it seemed others did, too, as my email list grew quite large.

Upon my return to the United States, another dear 86-year old friend, Marian Feniger, whose literary judgement I trust, insisted I publish my dispatches. With no formal publishing experience beyond financial research reports written at various investment banks long ago, I chose to self-publish *Fifteen Feet from the Pope*. The book made a great Christmas gift to family and friends. It also received favorable feedback from another cherished friend, Susan Conroy, who presented the book to Marian Press.

For this new edition, titled, *Piazzas, Popes, and Pasta*, I expanded upon a number of my experiences, included more detail about why I chose to study theology, wrote about the classes themselves, and added an afterword describing my post-Rome life.

It has been over three years since my return and rarely does a day pass that I do not think about my Rome sojourn or interact with someone I met there. Time has made me increasingly appreciative of how blessed I was to be able to savor and soak up a unique place that begs to be explored.

Time and prayer have also given me greater insight as to why God may have called me to Rome. Much of my professional and apostolic work, and my personal relationships, are now rooted in, or colored by, those four months in Rome.

My hope and prayerful intention are that these pages may serve as a nudge of encouragement for you, dear reader, to act upon a risky inspiration from the Holy Spirit. God gives so much to those who follow Him with abandon. But, if nothing else, may these words provide a bit of joy and insight into an extraordinary city at the heart of Jesus Christ's precious gift to the world, the Catholic Church.

Luanne D. Zurlo
December 12, 2017
Feast Day of Our Lady of Guadalupe

Introduction

Before I embarked on a four-month sabbatical to Rome in late September 2013, a few friends asked me to email them my impressions of Rome and recount some of my experiences. One friend, Sarah, was even more specific, asking that I write about seemingly mundane, daily things, such as my favorite flavor of gelato, so she could vicariously experience this special moment I had been given.

I had never written publicly about myself and have shied away from Facebook and most other social media platforms, except for an infrequent tweet. But I was fully cognizant of how fortunate I was to spend four months in such an incredible city, so, in gratitude and discomfort, I started writing to a small list of friends and family with no promises as to frequency, length, or quality. The list grew and grew, to some 150 friends and family, and I ultimately wrote seventeen emails, which I called dispatches, published here with only minor editing.

Twenty years of intense, travel-heavy work led me to make the decision to step back and take an extended break from what had become an unbearable grind for me. I spent over nine years working as an equity analyst on Wall Street, covering Latin American and US telecommunications companies during the telco-tech boom and bust of the late 1990s and early 2000s. It was extraordinarily interesting and challenging work requiring top-level performance, long hours, and lots of travel. Most of the people I met along the way were smart, inquisitive, hardworking, and honest people trying to do the best job they could. Many of them became close friends.

Then 9/11 happened. I was downtown, working on the 46th floor of Goldman Sachs, a few blocks south of the World Trade Center, when the planes struck. The experience led me to reassess my priorities and gave me the courage to leave Wall Street a few months later.

Touched by the poverty I observed on my many trips throughout Latin America and dumbstruck by how poor the education levels were in the region, I went on to found and lead a nonprofit organization called Worldfund (www.worldfund.org), whose mission is to raise educational quality by providing intensive training for public school teachers and principals. After 11 years of building Worldfund, which required lots of travel between the headquarters in New York City and two subsidiaries in Brazil and Mexico, I was exhausted.

I decided in early 2013 to step back from the day-to-day management of Worldfund and seek my successor. It was a difficult decision. What gave me solace was Pope Benedict XVI's abdication announcement on Monday, February 11, 2013, the same day I had planned to tell the Worldfund board about my decision. I was heartbroken that Pope Benedict would no longer be our pope. But the news also gave me the idea that if the pope could step down, I could too!

In early March 2013, the week before the papal conclave which elected Pope Francis, I spent a week in Rome on a tour led by Dr. Timothy O'Donnell, president of Christendom College, and a close friend of our family. While there it became obvious to me, in a hard-to-describe interior way, that I needed to spend an extended period of time in Rome. Having studied a year in Bologna, Italy, nearly 25 years earlier, Italy was very familiar to me.

Long fascinated by theology, but having never formally studied it, I decided to structure my Rome sojourn around a couple of theology courses I arranged to audit at the Angelicum, a Pontifical University in Rome run by the Order of Preachers, God's precocious dogs, the Dominicans. Registration for the fall semester was held during the last week of September, so that is when I decided to arrive.

This is the origin of my dispatches from Rome.

Luanne D. Zurlo
May 12, 2014
First anniversary of the canonization of the
Martyrs of Otranto, including Capitano Francesco Zurlo

First Impressions

Arrival

No problems boarding my JFK-outbound plane, despite three overweight bags chock-full of books, or getting a taxi driver at Rome's Fiumicino Airport to drive me right up to my new front door on a beautiful, pedestrian street in the heart of Trastevere. My address is Via della Scala 17, a 25-minute walk to both the Vatican and to the Angelicum, located just north of the Roman forum.

I arrived about nine in the morning and sat on one of my suitcases, watching the morning routine of the neighborhood unfold until 10 a.m. or so, when I was scheduled to meet the owner of my apartment, Renato. Renato, who speaks perfect English, was very helpful and responsive leading up to my arrival and subsequently throughout my stay. I have nothing but positive things to say about Airbnb, the online platform on which I found my apartment.

The most difficult part of my arrival was hauling my stuff up to my new, fourth-floor apartment, requiring a 73-step climb. My goal is not to huff and puff at the top by the time I leave at the end of January, even carrying a few gallons of water and groceries!

Trastevere is sort of like the Greenwich Village of Rome, old and quaint with winding cobblestone streets and lots of nightlife and restaurants. Thankfully, despite the bustle on the streets below, my small apartment is quiet and flooded with great light and has two small outdoor terraces where one can enjoy wonderful views. My good luck continued, as I easily located an Italian-style coffee maker in the kitchen, which makes fantastic strong coffee, much needed after my overnight flight.

After unpacking, I pulled out my map on which I had already marked the route I would walk to arrive at Largo Angelicum 1, the conspicuous address of the Angelicum itself. I chose the Angelicum for two reasons. It is the one Pontifical University that offers most of its classes in English, and it is run by Dominicans, the all-star theologians among Catholic religious orders.

What brought me to one of the premier centers of Catholic theology?

Though a cradle Catholic, I never attended Catholic schools. The extent of my formal "theological" training was 1970s-quality Wednesday afternoon CCD class. *Kumbaya* has become a clichéd reference to the vapidity of Catholic religious instruction that permeated American dioceses in the 70s and 80s. I was a child of this era. I cannot remember what I eat for breakfast on most days, but I can sing every stanza of *Kumbaya* on cue.

I was thoroughly comfortable studying and working among smart, accomplished people for whom faith was either anathema or else had little importance, as this was my natural environment for most of my life. What piqued my growing curiosity in Catholicism was meeting bright, accomplished people for whom their Christian faith was a priority, a defining force in their lives. As a whole, they seemed a whole lot happier or, at least conveyed a sense of peace. Peace and joy are not the first two adjectives I would choose to describe many today.

My curiosity, inspired by the Holy Spirit I'm sure, led me to explore the profound and beautiful foundations of my Catholic faith that, admittedly, I had taken for granted. I started to read Catholic authors and I asked many questions to people who had a profound understanding of the Catholic faith. My yearning to learn about the faith in a more serious and systematic way, along with my realization that it was possible to be a part-time student at a renowned university in the heart of the Catholic world, led me to taking that first 25-minute, uphill walk to Largo Angelicum 1, on that hot, late September day.

Registration for the fall semester, starting in early October, ends tomorrow, Friday, September 27, so I figured I should get there today. Registration definitely lives up to the have-to-do-things-in-person Italian meme. Having studied the slightly less-than-clear university website, I concluded that I fit into the category of *simpliciter extraordinarii* (non-degree students) which required that I bring to registration a signed registration form, a certificate of formerly completed studies, a letter from a priest vouching for me, and two passport-sized photos. In my overnight-travel, sleep-deprived state, it did not occur to me to bring my passport. And probably a good thing, as I have a proclivity to lose it, having done so twice before while traveling abroad. The war-weary registrars let the passport thing slide, completed my registration, and were unexpectedly nice throughout the hour-long process.

So, for just over $600 I will audit two classes, one on the theology of St. Thomas Aquinas and the other on spiritual theology, offered by two well-known Dominican professors, Father Wojciech Giertych, Theologian of the Papal Household, and Father Paul Murray, a well-known poet and preacher.

Apart from these weekly academic classes, which meet on Tuesdays from 10:30 a.m.–12:15 p.m., Wednesdays from 8:30–10:15 a.m., and Fridays from 9:30–10:15 a.m., my plan is to spend my time walking and reading a lot, with no air travel, and very little travel outside of Rome.

I spent my first evening entertaining some friends who were vacationing in Rome and were returning home the following morning. What a blessing to spend my first night in Rome with three wonderful American women.

Behind Vatican Walls to Discuss Finance and Economics

I woke up early my second day in Rome with the rare opportunity to pass through the Vatican walls to attend a conference entitled, "The Debt Crisis, Financial Reform, and the Common Good," held in a beautiful conference center located in the middle of the Vatican Gardens. The invitation-only conference was organized by Fondazione Centesimus Annus Pro Pontifice, and I received an invitation because of my teaching position at Catholic University of America (CUA).

The conference provided a sudden reintroduction into the contrasting mindsets and styles of Europeans and Americans. I have been working primarily with Latin Americans in recent years, so I have less of a familiarity with the European mindset, specifically the Italian one. I had lived in various European countries as a child and young adult for a combined total of some five years, but this was years ago and did not involve discussions about finance and economics.

Major segments of Latin America's population have embraced free-market capitalism over the last twenty to thirty years, with a few notable exceptions. Those who look honestly at the data cannot deny that Latin American countries that have pursued more free-market-oriented policies have experienced more robust economic growth and poverty reduction than the small handful of Latin American countries that have not.

I was struck by the skepticism toward capitalism and free markets expressed subtly and sometimes not so subtly by the Italian economists and Vatican officials participating in the conference. The roots of this skepticism run deep, some believing that they stem from perhaps as far back as the Middle Ages, when economic activity was organized around a top-down, more restrictive, paternalistic guild system.

Since Pope Leo XIII's famous encyclical, *Rerum Novarum* (*Rights and Duties of Capital and Labor*) — published in 1891 in response to the contrasting evils of socialism and abhorrent working conditions resulting from the Industrial Revolution — the Catholic Church has spoken consistently and eloquently about the need for capital to be subservient to the wellbeing of the human person as opposed to the human person being a slave to capital.

Treating people, including higher-paid, white-collar workers, in a utilitarian, expendable way in the single-minded pursuit of profits is a modern manifestation of this mindset. Each and every pope since Pope Leo XIII has spoken out against the dehumanizing potential of both socialism and a heartless form of capitalism.

In recent years unfettered capitalism has been blamed by many in the Church hierarchy for spawning extreme consumerism. After the fall of the Berlin Wall in November 1989 and the collapse of the Soviet Union in December 1991, Pope John Paul II presciently warned the formerly communist nations against replacing the cloak of materialistic socialism with that of materialistic consumerism.

On the one hand, for those who view American free-market capitalism in positive terms, responsible for generating economic growth and material wellbeing for the greatest share of citizens over the past two centuries, it is hard to understand how capitalism can be viewed with such skepticism.

On the other hand, an honest look at how so many are treated in the workplace, including seemingly comfortable white-collar places of work, and at how shopping has become such an all-consuming focus for so many, can help us understand where some of the skepticism toward capitalism comes from.

Those who criticize American-style capitalism might take a more honest look at their own systems, how stubbornly high unemployment rates and lack of economic growth in Italy, France, and Greece, owing to burdensome, anti-free-market state control and corruption, have created their own set of inhumane outcomes.

One element of American-style capitalism that I did not hear criticized among the conference participants, including those from the Vatican, is our generosity. Americans are extraordinarily generous, and the Vatican shows no reticence in accepting American, capitalism-generated donations.

One of the conclusions some of us drew from the conference talks was that debt at all levels — whether for individuals, financial institutions, or governments — was, and continues to be, a difficult challenge weakening our financial systems and broader economies. The vast accumulation of debt has both ethical and technical roots, neither of which has been adequately addressed. I believe the Catholic Church has a role to play in drawing attention to the ethical and moral implications of unsustainable high debt at every level.

My Neighborhood Church, Missing a Caravaggio

The Sunday after my arrival, I made a wonderful discovery: Chiesa Santa Maria della Scala located on the piazza right outside my door. It is a stunningly beautiful, Baroque-to-the-hilt, yet warm church run by the Discalced Carmelite nuns, an order founded by St. Teresa of Avila, one of my favorite saints. The church contains a number of beautiful paintings depicting St. Teresa and St. John of the Cross. A special, closed-off chapel behind the main altar, houses the right foot of St. Teresa, preserved in a beautiful reliquary on top of an altar.

Santa Maria della Scala was built between 1593 and 1610 at the site of a miracle attributed to the Virgin Mary. As the story goes, the mother of a dying child fervently prayed in front of a painting of the Virgin Mary and baby Jesus which was hanging under the stairs, *scala*, of an apartment building, the spot where the church now stands. The child miraculously recovered. This very same painting is venerated at a side altar of the church where people come to write prayer petitions on a little pad, located in front of the painting, tossing these petitions onto a pile at the foot of the painting.

Today the church is known better for something else: having rejected a Caravaggio painting. It was either the Carmelite superior of the former convent connected to the church or the local cardinal who contracted Caravaggio's famous *Death of the Virgin* for one of the church's half-dozen chapels. The painting was rejected and found its way to the Louvre because the model Caravaggio used for the Virgin was widely thought to be Caravaggio's prostitute mistress.

I attended 11:30 a.m. Sunday Mass, and when it started, only three of us were in the pews. By the Gospel reading, some 10 others had joined us, a firsthand experience of the anemic Mass attendance in Italy that I had heard about. The church offers daily Mass and Adoration once a week, which I am thrilled about. The bells at this church, and other nearby churches, ring every hour and between the top of every hour, a rare sound in the United States today. This means no sleeping in late while in Rome.

A Few Other Impressions from My First Days in Rome

The other regular sounds I hear from my apartment are of playing children, as there is a nursery school right next to my apartment building. So, while one normally does not see many small children in Italy, in my neighborhood I do. Oh, and lots of dogs! Like New York City, Rome is a city of dog lovers. But unlike New York City, it seems most restaurants and other establishments allow dogs inside. And compared to New Yorkers, Romans are less fastidious about cleaning up after their dogs.

Unless one travels overseas it can be difficult to appreciate how extraordinarily important relative exchange rates are to the wallet. Because the value of the Euro is strong against the dollar, prices seem very expensive to me. If one exchanges U.S. dollars (in cash) for Euros, the price of one Euro is a whopping $1.50. By making purchases on my American Express credit card, which does not charge foreign exchange (FX) transaction fees, I get a $1.35 rate, so I will try to purchase as much as I can on my credit card. Euro prices are more or less equal to U.S. dollar prices, but given the weaker dollar, this actually makes Euro prices 35 percent more expensive than U.S. prices. Thus far, I have noticed that only coffee, wine, and olive oil are relative bargains.

For the weather buffs out there, it has been spectacular — warm, sunny, and in the high seventies. One of the apartments in my building has an umbrella holder outside the front door with about a dozen umbrellas, so I have expectations of a serious rainy season.

I've discovered a number of fantastic classical music concerts from my online exploration, many of which are free performances at various churches. Live classical music is another activity that I look forward to, starting with two Rachmaninoff concerts next week at the National Music Academy, appropriately named Santa Cecilia, in honor of the patron saint of music.

Fifteen Feet from the Pope

I came within fifteen feet of Pope Francis yesterday! Thankfully, I didn't read the "rules" before heading over to Piazza San Pietro (St. Peter's Square) yesterday morning to attend the pope's Wednesday audience. One "rule" is that one is supposed to present a (free) ticket to enter the square. This message didn't seem to reach the well-muscled security guards who let everyone in, ticket or not. I suspect there must be a special gym near the Vatican with miraculous, muscle-building powers where the St. Peter's Square security guards work out, as all the ones I noticed have perfect, self-pleasing shapes under their form-fitting uniforms and requisite Ray-Bans.

Watching Pope Francis live for the first time was an extraordinary experience. I consider myself pope privileged, as I have had the opportunity to stand very close to Saint John Paul II, shake Pope Emeritus Benedict XVI's hand, when he was Cardinal Ratzinger, and attend Mass celebrated by Pope Benedict in Havana, Cuba. Each of these encounters was unforgettable, and seeing Pope Francis yesterday was no different. The pope rolled into St. Peter's at 9:50 a.m. atop his open Popemobile. It took thirty minutes to ride around the square, kissing babies and waving to the ecstatic crowds.

Some observations. Pope Francis smiled authentically the entire thirty minutes, as one can view up close the proceedings as they are televised on two huge screens at two

21

corners in the square. Smiling nonstop is not easy. The pope truly seemed to enjoy himself and derive great energy from the outpouring of love. He must have kissed at least 75 babies on his loop and, amazingly, only three of them cried. I was impressed by the calm of the babies, as I can imagine how frightening it would be for one to be quickly handed over to a security guy, and then foisted up in order to be kissed by a big man in white. I was also impressed by the security guy who does most of the baby duty. He clearly has developed an effective baby-foisting technique, right hand under the bottom, as if balancing a basketball right before the shot, and left hand on the baby's stomach to balance.

Pope Francis then hopped out of the Popemobile and energetically scaled the steps leading to the platform from which he spoke. (I have become obsessed with steps because of the 73 I have to climb to my apartment.) This pope clearly does not like to keep to script. The style of his commentary on one of St. Paul's letters suggests that he wrote it himself. Yet he still looked up from his notes on a number of occasions to add an even more personal, unscripted touch to his address. It was on these occasions when the audience was most enthralled, bursting into cheers. For me, the most powerful moment of his meditation was when, in extolling the beauty and sacredness of the Catholic Church even in the face of all her problems, Pope Francis said, "Men are sinners. Women are sinners." He then looked up from his paper, toward the cardinals seated at his left and said, "These cardinals are sinners; bishops are sinners; priests are sinners. I am a sinner; you are sinners." The crowd loved it, especially the cardinal part.

It occurred me that Francis is a pope who appeals to the heart, and people are so hungry for their hearts to be touched at this moment. Pope Benedict — considered by some to be one of the most brilliant popes that ever lived — was more a pope of the head. Pope Benedict's first encyclical, *Deus Caritas Est* (*God is Love*) gives a sense of both Benedict's heart and head, but his communication style was more cerebral. Head and heart are both equally critical to a well-formed person, but sometimes one needs to be emphasized over the other, at least it seems to me.

It was during the moments in which Pope Francis looked up and out into the audience that he most effectively touched our hearts. My Italian is rudimentary, but I got much more out of Pope Francis's remarks in Italian than I did from the American priest who then summarized the remarks in English. The remarks were summarized one by one by priests speaking French, German, Arabic, Polish, Spanish, and a heavily Carioca-accented Portuguese. The summaries were formulaic, with lots of fancy words that create a veil over the raw meaning. The pope's language is simple and penetrating.

A "Perfect" Meal

After leaving St. Peter's Square, I had a fantastic surprise! After being on my feet for many hours in the sun, I was tired and hungry. I crossed Ponte Sant'Angelo (Angel Bridge) into Centro Storico and happened upon Alfredo e Ada (Via dei Banchi Nuovi, 14) the proverbial hole-in-the-wall, traditional restaurant with only five tables and no menu. On a trip to Rome 13 years ago, I had come upon this same restaurant and had one of my most memorable meals there and never could find it again, as I never noted the name and this is not the sort of place that has a card, let alone a website. I had just as memorable a meal yesterday, and all for 20 euros — pasta cooked perfectly with a simple *pomodoro* sauce, which was out of this world, *braciole* (though, I must say, my mother's is slightly better) a side dish of a spinach-like vegetable sautéed in garlic and olive oil, and a choice of table wine, red or white. I chose the red and finished off the meal with a fantastic round cookie that the owner insisted I dip in the red wine.

A Bernini Discovery

One of the best things about touring blind — just following one's nose and not reading ahead about what one is about to see — is being totally surprised by something that touches your senses without any forewarning or expectation. This past Monday morning, I decided to explore my new Trastevere neighborhood by just wandering the streets.

I came upon Chiesa di San Francesco d'Assisi a Ripa, where St. Francis is said to have spent time. Here one can view the rock that he used as his pillow. Yes, rock — he was definitely different than us. Tomorrow, October 4, is the feast day of St. Francis, a major holiday in Italy, as St. Francis is one of Italy's two patron saints. He is also the namesake of Pope Francis, who will spend the day in Assisi tomorrow.

Saint Catherine of Siena is Italy's other patron saint and, like the indefatigable St. Teresa de Avila, St. Catherine was a strong, courageous woman and a doctor of the Church. She exhorted Pope Gregory XI, in person, to buck up and return the papacy from Avignon to Rome in the late 14th century. She also pushed for reform of the clergy and administration of the Papal States, all before her untimely death at age 33. I think Pope Francis could use a modern-day St. Catherine.

Back to my discovery. San Francesco d'Assisi is a nondescript church relative to Rome standards. But then, unexpectedly, discretely situated in a side chapel to the left of the main altar, I came upon one of Bernini's last works, a statue of Beata Ludovica Albertoni. Incredible! I was blown away and knew this must be a major work, but the lighting was poor and the description plate difficult to read so it wasn't until I arrived home and looked it up that I discovered that this was a Bernini statue, finished in 1674 when the artist was 75 years old. Blessed Ludovica was a noblewoman who lived in the mid-16th century. Following the death of her husband while she was in her thirties, she became a Third Order Franciscan at this very church. Ludovica is buried under the Bernini-sculpted funeral monument, which captures the moment before she died, reflecting both pain and ecstasy. Bernini's *Ecstasy of St. Teresa* is much better known, created twenty years earlier. Both are truly remarkable. I was proud to read that Gian Lorenzo Bernini was born in Naples, where the Zurlo clan comes from.

As I write this, I am compelled to continue the what-I-hear-from-my-apartment theme. Every evening starting at 7:40, I hear a live accordionist play a rotation of four songs in Piazza della Scala: "O Sole Mio," "Volare," the Godfather theme song, and another "Italian" classic, "Besame Mucho." From what I can tell, most of the American and German tourists eating in Piazza della Scala would lose the Sesame Street game, "Which one of these four does not belong?"

Che sarà sarà

An Unexpected Pope Sighting

Sunday I learned a lesson in letting go, *che sarà sarà*. After a week of home cooking, I was eager to eat a great meal at a great restaurant. I planned to eat at a friend-recommended restaurant and then check out a famed chocolateria-gelateria in a neighborhood I hadn't yet explored on this trip — Piazza del Popolo/Piazza di Spagna — the Upper East Side of Rome, where all the great designer shops are located and where the "beautiful people" hang. I have been given precious new insight into friends based on the location and characteristics of their restaurant recommendations. First on the agenda, Sunday Mass at St. Peter's and then my eagerly anticipated *pranzo* (lunch) and first gelato.

I attended a beautiful Latin Mass, accompanied by the Sistine Chapel Choir, also known as the Pope's Choir, which sounded angelic. There must have been fifty priests and cardinals officiating and lots of incense. After saying the Our Father, the priest often asks people to extend a greeting of peace to those around them. I had never appreciated this moment in Mass as much as I did this Sunday. From the various words expressed for peace, or the accent spoken, it was obvious that those around me came from many different countries — Poland, Spain, the United States, Italy, Mexico, and Germany. It struck me just how unifying the Catholic Mass is. With its very defined structure, we were all able to actively participate without necessarily understanding each spoken word. There seemed to be no national barriers between us during the Mass.

Then a big surprise! I exited the doors of St. Peter's a few minutes before noon to a see an unexpected sea of people in the square, just like during the Wednesday papal audience. The two big screens were set up, and there was a large banner hanging from a high window in the building to the left of the square, where the papal apartment is, the one in which Pope Francis is not living. At noon sharp, Pope Francis stepped up to the window and addressed the crowds, to great cheers. He then began to pray the Angelus, a prayer in honor of the Virgin Mary, with the participation of the people in the square.

Next, Pope Francis spoke to the crowds in his informal manner for about five to eight minutes, focusing his remarks on faith and how difficult it can be to both have and keep the faith. He prayed, *Il Senor, credere la noi fede*. He then asked the crowd to repeat after him three times, "Lord, grow our faith." After this, Pope Francis asked us to pray for something, which I did not understand, during a moment of silence. The whole square was absolutely silent for about thirty seconds. It was remarkable to be among thousands and thousands of people in total silence. Pope Francis has an extraordinary ability to connect with people.

Another word about Vatican security guards. The inside guys do not belong to the same gym as the outside guys, or perhaps they aren't as diligent with respect to gym duty. But what the inside guards do have is the ability to manage crowds and distinguish between those who want to pray and those who just want to take pictures. St. Peter's is not a museum; it is an active basilica with many Masses offered, especially on Sunday. So, at defined moments, the guards have to quickly erect or dismantle barriers between different parts of the cathedral, amid hordes of people milling about.

And they have to make judgment calls as to whom to let through barriers to attend Mass or Confession or the special prayer chapel, and whom to hold back.

Searching for Caravaggio

The unexpected Pope Francis experience was a huge positive *che sarà sarà* moment. What followed was more challenging. I took the metro to Piazza del Popolo and decided first to make a quick pre-lunch visit to Santa Maria del Popolo, home to two major Caravaggios — *Conversion on the Way to Damascus* and the *Crucifixion of St. Peter*. I love Caravaggio and hope to see every Caravaggio in Rome during my stay.

Finding major works of art (or whatever) in Rome can be an art unto itself. The-harder-it-is-to-find-the-more-you-will-appreciate-it seems to be the animating theme behind the signage in Rome. I finally found the chapel where the two Caravaggio's are hung, in almost complete darkness, on two less visible sidewalls. I plopped a Euro in the lighting machine and — nothing. The lighting mechanism did not work. Argh! I took a deep, calming breath and turned to walk out, knowing I could and would come back.

Here's an interesting fact I learned while writing this. Caravaggio painted two St. Paul conversion paintings, the first one being *The Conversion of St. Paul* that is housed in the Odescalchi Balbi Collection in Rome. It is not entirely clear why the second painting for Santa Maria del Popolo was commissioned right after the first one, possibly by the same cardinal. From studying the online versions, I like the image at Santa Maria del Popolo better. It feels more powerful and true to life. Here is a guy who just experienced something miraculous, yet personal, and the horse and companion in front of the horse are depicted as if, ho hum, nothing out of the ordinary going on here. Isn't that often the case in life: something that has a great impact on you leaves those around you relatively untouched?

The Emperor of Fettuccine to the Rescue

I was hungry and tired and ready for a fabulous lunch. My intended destination was Il Due Ladroni, a restaurant about which by my guide book commented: "Italian gossip mags always feature a few grainy photos of celebs dining at this classy but unpretentious restaurant." So there I headed, in my sharp, Italian-looking outfit. After a 10-minute walk south from Piazza del Popolo, I arrived, only to find it closed. *Va bene.* No problem. I had the hunger of a wolf (*ho fame come lupo*), but I decided to take it in stride.

As a fallback option, I decided to go to this same friend's other recommendation in the same neighborhood, Il Gusto, a more modern, multi-restaurant kind of place under beautiful old arches. This friend is obviously a "beautiful people" person. It is located across the street from *Ara Pacis* (Altar of Peace), an ancient altar built in tribute to Emperor Augustus housed in a (I will say it), ugly Richard Meier modern museum that looks completely out of place. Il Gusto was packed with young, trendy, very handsome couples and families and was totally booked, with a free table not likely to become available for longer than my hunger would allow.

I continued my search to find, now, a non-friend-recommended restaurant. I came upon Alfredo III: The Emperor of Fettuccine. Alfredo III is one of those old-time, somewhat high-end, local neighborhood restaurants. It is a magnet for non-cutting-edge celebrities willing to have their meal permanently commemorated with a photo on the wall, and is managed by a larger-than-life owner and a crew of waiters who have worked there for years. We have a number of these on the Upper East Side of New York. The food is very good, but not cheap, in this restaurant genre.

The restaurant website photo gallery captures the essence of Alfredo III, except for one thing. It is missing the can't-be-missed photo of Gérard Depardieu stuffing his own face with a fist full of Fettuccine Alfredo.

There was lovely outdoor terrace seating. But this seating was reserved for Italians. Non-Italians were relegated to indoor seating. I actually didn't mind coach class seating, as it was cool inside and I was guided to a table right next to a large window through which I could unobtrusively observe the glamorous, first-class, outdoor-seated Italians. The ratio of Italians to non-Italians was about 4:1, and that made me very pleased.

My first important Roman restaurant thesis is: real Italians frequent restaurants far from tourist spots and, therefore, without spectacular views. The corollary being: one generally has to make a "location versus quality-authenticity" choice in restaurants. Despite the non-Italian celebrity photos, Alfredo III fell in the latter category, and I enjoyed the absolute best *scaloppine di vitello al vino bianco e funghi* (veal) that I have ever eaten. *Buonissimo!*

My First Gelato

Onward and upward to my first gelato of the trip! Venchi — an upscale chocolate and gelato place on Via della Croce 25, between Via del Corso and the Spanish Steps — was my destination because I had received a generous Venchi gift card in appreciation for taking care of Queen Ruby, a neurotic, miniature Dachshund (are there any other kind?) for a week this past August. While I will admit to having a Dachshund fixation, it does not negate the fact that I have observed only two breeds of dogs residing in Rome: Dachshunds and mutts.

There was a mob of people in front of the counter so I couldn't read the uniquely Italian flavors. Accordingly, I had to shout out flavors I knew. As a chocolate lover, my verdict was that the Venchi chocolate-flavored gelato was fantastic, better than the pistachio and coconut flavors that I also chose. But when it comes to regular chocolate, I have had better. In my opinion, the Swiss and Belgians retain their chocolate-making superiority over the Italians.

Since milk and my digestive system are not on friendly terms, I am being judicious in my gelato indulgences. My first rule: never eat gelato at a place whose pistachio gelato is bright green colored, a sure sign of artificial stuff thrown in. Venchi's pistachio gelato was not green and was delicious, but the chocolate was truly memorable. Definitely worth a return visit. I haven't yet come up with any other gelato rules but will divulge them as they develop.

Observations

Various Observations from My Daily Walks

I have yet to walk home the same way twice, even when I have tried to do so. There are just too many tiny, winding streets on which to get lost in Centro Storico, which is only minutes away from my apartment. Normally I keep my eyes focused downward so as not to trip on the cobblestone streets. But during one of my walks home last week, I happened to look up right at a placard indicating that it was Giuseppe Verdi's home, not far from the Parliament Building near Via del Corso. I searched for information about Verdi's Roman home on the Internet back at my apartment but found absolutely nothing about it, only an un-user-friendly website about Verdi and a few festivities celebrating his 200th birthday anniversary, which had just happened. Italian websites or, rather, the lack of commercial establishment websites, is a whole other topic.

I have learned that opera in Rome is not great, especially when the New York Metropolitan is your point of reference. However, I am hopeful to get to La Scala in Milan. I've never experienced anyone booing a performer at an opera. I understand this happens on occasion at La Scala. While I do not relish listening to a subpar performance, I think experiencing such an honest reaction by a normally staid audience ensemble would be intriguing. From my understanding, the Germans are even more brutal in their immediate feedback.

American opera audiences are more willing to politely applaud even a subpar performance, though I can truly say I have never heard a bad performance at the Metropolitan Opera. As a proud New Yorker, I think the Met is the best opera house in the world.

I had another sighting of a famous artist's home yesterday, near the Spanish Steps. Sigrid Undset, an author I have long been meaning to read, lived in Rome for nearly two years around 1920. She won the Nobel Prize in Literature for her trilogy, *Kristin Lavransdatter*. I just learned that she also wrote a biography of Catherine of Siena.

Another memorable *passeggiata* experience. I had the best cannoli that I have ever eaten at a Sicilian pastry shop, Dolce Nonna Vincenza, located only eight minutes from my apartment on foot. I would choose a cannoli over a gelato any day under 85 degrees Fahrenheit.

Thanks to my heightened observation mode, over the past week or so I've observed Roman street scenes that most likely would have passed me by back in the United States.

Just around the corner from my apartment in Trastevere, I caught sight of a robust, perhaps *gorda*, fully habited nun strolling down a street licking one of the biggest gelato cones I have ever seen, with a huge smile on her face. This put just as wide a smile on my own face, something about a religious taking such joy out of a simple pleasure.

One morning I was almost knocked over by two men, arms wrapped around each other's shoulders, crammed together in a tiny, street-cleaning vehicle, laughing as they whipped around Via Garibaldi, right around the corner from my apartment. I am not sure if the shoulder embrace was due to the very tight quarters or just a gesture of sheer joy in cleaning streets.

Bemused observations have led to two conclusions:

First, about half the people snapping photos don't truly imbibe the subject of their effort. Instead, the drill is frame, focus, snap, and then on to the next sight. While I may be sorry, I've instituted a no-camera policy on my sabbatical. I also carry no cell phone since my four-month sabbatical extends to portable electronic devices. On a few, limited occasions I plan to bring along my iPad and snap a couple of key, meaningful places. I find that I appreciate things more deeply without a camera to distract me. Hopefully the really good stuff will stay in my brain.

Second, it is truly remarkable the lengths to which young women will go when posing for photos. The drill here seems to be yoga-like contortion pose, run to the person snapping (usually boyfriend or husband), inspect photo, delete, and repeat until satisfied. I observe that women of a certain age, and men in general, do not pose.

Believe it or not, it has been challenging to find a garlic press here. The first one I came across in a designer kitchen store actually cost $40. I finally found a more modestly designed one at a street vendor, but it doesn't work well, and I am hoping one of my visiting friends/family might take note.

Roman bus maps must be designed by vindictive, sick people! Absolutely incomprehensible. Blind experiential learning (just do it and make lots of mistakes) is how I am figuring out the bus system. After a slow start with a number of jump-off-quick-and-take-the-next-returning-bus-back-to-where-I-started attempts, I have now figured out four various bus routes that are particularly useful — the H, 65, 271, and 40. I first took the H from the central Termini station, where nearly every bus in Rome starts or ends its route. Asking for the H bus stop was a lesson in humility, since I had forgotten how to say "H" in Italian. Word to the wise, the Spanish "aahchay" doesn't work with Italians. My lingering moral dilemma: Must I get my bus ticket validated when the bus is so crowded that I cannot get near the validating machine? I was feeling okay not doing so, until witnessing numerous American tourists go to great lengths moving through crowds to have them validated (i.e., stamped by a machine). An impressive show of honesty. I have yet to see a single Italian validate a ticket on the bus.

Homemaking Lessons

I just learned an important new Italian word, *ammorbidente*. I finally summoned the nerve to wash my first load of clothes in the washing machine located in my kitchen. Figuring out how to use the machine itself ended up being the easy part. Being a New Yorker, I am used to complicated, front-loading European-style washing machines that take three hours to clean a load of clothes. It was deciphering all the photo-less detergent/cleaning supply bottles stored under my kitchen sink, which was my undoing. Rather proud of myself when the spin cycle ended, I unloaded what turned out to be a load of not-quite-clean but thoroughly fabric-softened clothes. This was a case where I wished I had done a pre- versus post-dictionary check.

Another kitchen lesson I learned during this first week cooking for myself in Rome involved Puttanesca seasoning. I have little patience for learning what spice is good for what dish, so I tend to stick with garlic and salt, which I think tastes good on practically everything. I came across a rather large bag of Puttanesca seasoning near the checkout counter during one of my first food-shopping expeditions. I bought it, thinking it would spruce things up a bit. Lesson learned: two tablespoons of Puttanesca seasoning in a pot of bean soup is one-and-a-half tablespoons too much.

Our Lady of Fatima, JPII, and Another Pope Francis Sighting

I had another Pope Francis sighting. The statue of Our Lady of Fatima, which rarely leaves Portugal, was flown to

Rome this past Saturday for about 48 hours. As background yesterday, October 13, 2013, was the 96th anniversary of the final Marian apparition that occurred near Fatima, Portugal. Mary appeared to three poor shepherd children every 13th day of the month from June through October in 1917. The two younger children, SS. Jacinta and Francisco Marto, passed away soon after the apparitions, and the third, Servant of God Lucia Santos, passed away in 2005 at the age of 97.

During the five apparitions leading up to the sixth and final October 13 apparition, Mary told the three children that a miracle would occur on October 13. Despite torrential rain, some 70,000 people were reported to have shown up to witness the miracle, including a number of news outlets. What they witnessed has come to be called the Miracle of the Sun, in which the sun danced in the sky and was able to be viewed directly by the human eye without blinding the person. Various-colored rays also emanated from the sun during its miraculous movements.

Pope John Paul II was shot in St. Peter's Square on May 13, 1981, the 64th anniversary of the first apparition. He came very close to death and attributed the saving of his life to Our Lady of Fatima. After John Paul II recovered, he commissioned a painting of the Virgin Mary on the corner wall of one of the brick buildings to the right of St. Peter's Square. Why? Right after he was shot, he searched for an image of Mary around St. Peter's Square and could not find one. He also made a pilgrimage to Fatima and brought the very same bullet that lodged in his chest from the gunshot. This bullet is now embedded in the crown of this same Our Lady of Fatima statue that was venerated by Pope Francis and carried in a procession around St. Peter's Square this past Saturday.

Pope Francis led a prayer service and Rosary with the statue in St. Peter's Square on Saturday afternoon. It was beautiful. The pope seemed tired, but by the very end of his remarks, he perked up a bit. Pope Francis offered a special 10:30 a.m. Mass yesterday (Sunday) in St. Peter's Square, which I watched live from my apartment, and again, I must say he seemed very tired to me. It is hard to imagine carrying his responsibilities at the age of 76. After the Mass, Pope Francis consecrated the world to the Immaculate Heart of Mary. Like Pope John Paul II and Pope Benedict, Pope Francis has a deep Marian devotion.

A Sad Moment in Rome's Past

Today, October 16, 2013, is the seventieth anniversary of the beginning of the brutal roundup of Roman Jews by the city's German Nazi occupiers who seized Rome after Mussolini's Fascist government fell in July 1943. Between 10,000 and 11,000 Jews lived in Rome in 1943, the vast majority in a ghetto located next to the Tiber River, across from Trastevere, where I live, and where Rome's Jews lived until the early Middle Ages.

Of these 10,000 to 11,000 Jews, 1,022 (including 200 children) were seized by Nazis in an early dawn raid on the morning of October 16, 1943, and sent to Auschwitz. Only sixteen survived, fifteen men and one woman. In all of Italy in 1943, there were an estimated 45,000 Jews, with a heavier concentration in the north. Of these 45,000 Jews, 6,806 were deported, 5,969 of whom were murdered, and 837 survived. Mid-Italy to the north came under Nazi occupation after Mussolini's fall and the south of Italy and islands came under Allied occupation.

Providentially (I don't believe in coincidences), I spent yesterday afternoon exploring the Jewish neighborhood of Rome, ate at a Jewish-Italian restaurant, and spent a few hours at the Museo Ebraico, connected to Rome's largest synagogue. Today, there are 16 synagogues in Rome and an estimated 12,000 to 13,000 Jews. Some 3,000 of Rome's Jews today are relatively recent émigrés or refugees from Libya.

I bought a book at the museum titled, *The Racial Laws and the Jewish Community of Rome 1938–1945*, which is where my figures come from. Reading this book, I learned that some 35 pieces of legislation against Italian Jews were approved by the Ministerial Council of Mussolini's government before the German occupation, starting in September 1938, as Mussolini was developing closer relations with Hitler, leading up to the Pact of Steel of 1939. Prior to yesterday, I had been under the impression that Italy's culpability with respect to how Jews were treated before and during World War II was limited to *after* the Nazi occupation.

Two weeks prior to the roundup, the Nazi SS had broken into the offices of the Roman Jewish Community and stole its registers and documents (and money), helping the Nazis identify the names and addresses of Roman Jews. Some 90 percent of Roman Jews found refuge in the homes of non-Jewish citizens, many from some of Rome's oldest and most prominent families, and in Rome's many convents and seminaries, in response to explicit requests by Pope Pius XII.

In Defense of Pope Pius XII

Pope Pius XII has been slandered mercilessly since his death in 1958. What many do not appear to appreciate is the extreme dilemma he faced. Pope Pius had two stark options: speak out assertively against the Nazis and their unspeakable brutality against the Jews, a tactic that had proven disastrous, or speak in more veiled terms and quietly, but aggressively work to physically save as many Jews as possible. Pius XII chose the second option and is excoriated for it.

Albrecht von Kessel, an official at the German Embassy to the Holy See during the war, and active in the anti-Nazi resistance, wrote in 1963, quoted in the Jewish Virtual Library, an online encyclopedia of Jewish history, politics and culture: "We were convinced that a fiery protest by Pius

XII against the persecution of the Jews ... would certainly not have saved the life of a single Jew. Hitler, like a trapped beast, would react to any menace that he felt directed at him, with cruel violence."

The Catholic clergy of Holland were the most vocal in their protest against Jewish persecutions. As a result, 79 percent of Dutch Jews were deported, more than anywhere else in Western Europe. A former inmate of Dachau, Msgr. Jean Bernard, later bishop of Luxembourg, wrote in *Priestblock 25487: A Memoir of Dachau*: "The detained priests trembled every time news reached us of some protest by a religious authority, but particularly by the Vatican. We all had the impression that our warders made us atone heavily for the fury these protests evoked." More than 8,000 Catholic priests in Germany came into open conflict with the Third Reich and were subsequently threatened, beaten, imprisoned, or killed by the regime, representing well over one-third of Germany's priests. I do not think many people know this.

Pius XII supervised a rescue network that saved an estimated 800,000-plus Jewish lives, more than all the international agencies put together. It is estimated that 60 to 65 percent of Europe's Jews were exterminated during World War II. "Only" 10 percent of Roman Jews were exterminated due, in large measure, to the efforts of Pope Pius XII.

Of the estimated ten to eleven thousand Jews living in Rome on the tragic morning of October 16, 1943, 1,022 were captured when the Nazis conducted a brutal roundup. Many Jews escaped capture thanks to a warning from the Vatican to Rome's chief rabbi, Israel Zolli, who later converted to Catholicism, taking the baptismal name Eugenio, Pope Pius XII's birth name.

Pope Pius XII had a deep love and appreciation for the Jews, as reflected in first-person accounts by many of the thousands of Roman Jews who found refuge behind Vatican walls, in Roman convents and seminaries, and in the Apostolic Palace of Castel Gandolfo, where smoke marks from cooking fires lit by Jewish refugees during the Nazi occupation remain today.

In appreciation of Pope Pius XII, Jewish refugees hidden in Castel Gandolfo presented him a large handmade cross after the war. Rather than display this cross in a more prominent location, like the Vatican Museum, Pope Pius XII asked that this cross remain in the basement of Castel Gandolfo to commemorate the Jews who suffered there.

After the end of World War II, Pius XII received a large delegation of Roman Jews to the Vatican, opening up the Imperial steps that are normally reserved for heads of state. He welcomed them warmly saying, "I am only the Vicar of Christ, but you are his very kith and kin."

Jewish historian, theologian, and Israeli diplomat Pinchas Lapide sums up Pius XII's role this way, in his book, *Three Popes and the Jews* (p. 266-267), Hawthorn, 1967: "Unable to cure the sickness of an entire civilization, and unwilling to bear the brunt of Hitler's fury, the Pope, unlike many far mightier than he, alleviated, relieved, retrieved, appealed, petitioned — and saved as best he could by his own lights. Who, but a prophet or a martyr could have done much more?"

Today, in Rome's main synagogue, commemorative services began at 5:30 a.m., the time at which the raid started. For anyone visiting Rome, I highly recommend visiting the Museo Ebraico. I also highly recommend the 1970 movie *Garden of the Finzi-Continis* about a bourgeois Jewish family leading up to World War II and their eventual deportation. I saw this movie about fifteen years ago and still remember it in great detail. *The Finzi-Continis*, along with Roberto Benigni's *Life Is Beautiful,* touchingly address the fate of Italian Jews in World War II.

A Roman Jewish Meal

To end this on a less-somber note, I will make mention of the terrific fried artichokes, *carciofi alla giudia*, I enjoyed for lunch at Ba'Ghetto, Via Portico d'Ottavia 57. More than 50 percent of the men eating there were wearing yarmulkes and, interestingly, most of these men were American. I ended up sitting next to a lovely Jewish American couple from Chicago who had just arrived in Rome the previous day. I soon realized that this is a destination restaurant for American Jews. As a NYC Upper West Sider, I felt right at home.

The one little dig I will make of the American tourists I have observed in Rome thus far is that most do not attempt to speak even a rudimentary word or phrase in Italian, such as *per favore* or *grazie*. The one thing I really appreciate about the tourist-fatigued Romans is that they really do indulge one's feeble attempts at speaking Italian. I cannot count the times a Roman merchant will start speaking English to me after enduring just a few words of my "Italian." But when I stick to my Italian, they go along with it, patiently. While Italy's neighbors to the west are overly maligned for their lack of *patience avec les Américains*, they certainly are not as linguistically accommodating as the Italians.

As a nod to my Brazilian friends, in addition to the fried artichokes, I also ordered the typical Roman Jewish dish, salted cod *baccala*, cooked Sicilian style. The *baccala* I have eaten in Brazil was better than what I had yesterday in Rome.

My Own Roman Holiday

This morning I rented a Vespa and whizzed around Rome. Without a doubt, this was one of the most harrowing and fun experiences I have had in a very long time! I was rather pleased with myself for conquering my initial fear, so I asked Francesco, the man who rented me the Vespa, to snap a photo of me before setting off.

I had happened upon Francesco's bike and Vespa rental shop by accident some two weeks ago while getting lost on the way to my first day of classes. One moment I was walking under a fantastically blue Roman sky, and the next moment I had to run for cover from a sudden torrential rain shower. This is how I found Francesco's bike rental business. While waiting for the rain to stop, he convinced me that renting a Vespa would be fun and *non c'è problema*.

I remained doubtful but couldn't get the idea out of my mind. What finally convinced me to give it a go was seeing the look of sheer fear on the faces of a group of German tourists trying to keep up with their Italian leader on Segways near Piazza Venezia a few days prior. I figured if these folks could ride Segways on the streets of Rome for what looked to be the first time, I could try a Vespa.

Despite our respective Italian-English language limitations, Francesco was able to explain to me how it worked. When it became obvious during his explanation that I wasn't an experienced Vespa pilot, or any sort of motorcycle kind of thing, he asked me point blank if I had actually ever ridden one. Figuring my answer could have important consequences I told him *certamente,* remembering that some 25 years ago I was a passenger on a Vespa while visiting Florence, with someone else driving. He did use the verb "ride" versus "drive," no? Francesco's confidence in me dissipated rapidly throughout the exchange, but finally he did let me wobble off, yelling from behind, *"Piano, piano!"* ("Slowly, slowly"). The first 20 minutes were sheer terror. But gradually, I got the hang of it and then loved every moment!

Having learned how to drive in Boston, I've seen just about every crazy and rude driving maneuver possible. Based on my four-hour Vespa experience, I will defend Roman drivers as superior to, and more accommodating than, Boston drivers! I took Francesco's *"piano, piano"* plea to heart and kept it very slow. Only twice was I beeped at for not going faster, by men in little sports cars.

The reaction my Vespa and I evoked was fascinating. Young men passing by in cars (everyone passed me) generally expressed looks of curiosity bordering on modest disgust, as my *piano* velocity must have represented a betrayal of the two-wheel motor class. Older men, however, seemed totally enamored with my Vespa. While stopped, either at a red light or during my three little breaks, older guys asked me what model of Vespa I was driving and whether it was automatic. Two men cited stories of past Vespas they owned. There seems to be a great appreciation for the machine.

My friend Diego, expert on all things Roman, informed me that Vespas evoked nostalgia, especially among older generations, since no one rides them anymore. Hearing this, I realized that, indeed, I had seen no other Vespas on the road during my ride! Rome has become a motorcycle city. Why? Motorcycles are faster than Vespas.

Curious, I learned that the first Vespa was produced right after the end of World War II, in 1946, by Piaggio &

Co., a former fighter plane manufacturer located near Pisa. Given the grim state of Italy's economy, the desperate need for an affordable mode of transportation, and poor road infrastructure, Enrico Piaggio, the founder's son, shifted the strategic direction of the company away from planes to Vespas. Enrico himself came up with the name. Upon seeing the first prototype, he is reputed to have exclaimed, "*Sembra una vespa!*" ("It looks like a wasp."). In the late 1940s, between 30,000 and 50,000 Vespas were sold annually. Thanks to *Roman Holiday,* a film starring Gregory Peck and Audrey Hepburn, which featured a brief Vespa ride, sales exploded, doubling to 100,000 in 1953 alone.

There is no better way to explore the outer reaches of Rome, or the hill areas, than on a Vespa. My first destination was the Aventine, the hill area above the Roman Forum. Following my nose and my limited Vespa turning ability, I came to a beautiful little square, Piazza dei Cavalieri di Malta, site of the famous Villa Malta keyhole, which provides a fantastic view of the Vatican. I had a vague memory of hearing about some famous keyhole in Rome. Since there was a line of about 10 people waiting to look through this keyhole, I decided it was worth checking out and rode right up to the keyhole gathering and abruptly stopped.

A lesson in humility was quickly meted out to me. I was able to turn off the motor without a problem. It was lifting the Vespa up and back to balance it on its kickstand that proved impossible for me. I am strong, but for the life of me I could not get the Vespa set upon its pesky kickstand so it would stay upright. Finally, a pitying older Italian man and his wife broke the line and came over offering help, which I readily accepted. The man then spent the next five minutes admiring my Vespa and told me about his old Vespa. Nostalgia.

St. Cecilia and the 1960 Olympic Village

From the Aventine, I rode along the Tiber toward the north of Rome to check out Rome's new major music venue, Auditorium Parco della Musica, which houses the famous Accademia Nazionale di Cecilia, the oldest music institution in the world, founded by papal bull in 1585. Saint Cecilia was a Roman noblewoman who was martyred in the third century AD and is one of the most venerated martyrs of Christian antiquity.

Legend has it that St. Cecilia was struck three times with a sword on her neck but didn't die for three days, during which she sang beautifully. She is the patron saint of musicians, poets, and church music, and her feast day is November 22. There is a hauntingly beautiful statue of St. Cecilia, with a neck wound, at the Church of St. Cecilia in my Trastevere neighborhood. I hope to attend a concert at the church on her feast day.

Next to the music auditorium is Rome's 1960 Olympic Village, which was purposefully built to be converted into residential housing after the Olympics. Every street is named after a different country. I loved the look and feel of this neighborhood. I later read that the area came under some disrepair in the 1980s, when an apartment could be purchased for about 20,000 euros. The neighborhood has been gentrified, partly due to the new world-class music auditorium. Apartments in the Olympic Village now go for half a million euros.

Riding Home

My four hours were starting to run out, so I headed home from this northern part of Rome, only to discover that when I got back to my Trastevere neighborhood, all the streets are one way. One doesn't take note of this when walking. Thankfully, the two motorcycle-mounted *Carabinieri* (members of an Italian military corps with police duties) who alerted me to this fact let me turn around with exasperated shrugs.

As I rolled up to Francesco's rental place, I noticed the gates were locked, so I parked the Vespa, having now figured out how to get it up on its kickstand after a few tries, and climbed the 73 steps up to my apartment to Skype with him (per my no-cell-phone policy), only to be told that he was in the middle of his pasta course and that I should come back in a few hours. I had assumed that he would have been eagerly awaiting his precious Vespa's return. Clearly, Francesco had other more important priorities at that moment.

Becoming Roman

This past week I made great strides on the path to becoming Roman. Since my Vespa adventure last Saturday, I stopped carrying the ubiquitous tourist badge of honor — *la pianta* (map). Rome is not an easy city to navigate. Unlike Renaissance architects, Roman city planners had an aversion to perpendicular angles. It is said that Boston's winding city streets are the remnant of meandering cow paths. I am reading the highly recommended book on Roman history, *Rome: A Cultural, Visual and Personal History*, by Robert Hughes. I still have not come to the part where the origins of Rome's jigsaw-puzzle-shaped road layout are explained.

Another becoming-Roman experience: Four different people asked me for directions this week, two of them Italian! Of course, I knew how to help the tourists because they want to get to spots that I, as a former tourist, had already been. It was the two Italians I could not help with an apologetic, *non lo so* ("I do not know").

And the most impressive test of being Roman — crossing the major arteries that merge into Piazza Venezia in front of the white wedding cake Vittorio Emanuele II monument next to the Roman Forum. This is a major road convergence point and one I have to pass three days a week on my way to class. Rules, and how they are enforced in Italy, require a dissertation unto itself, and I am sure many already have been written. From what I observe, the

expression "possession is nine-tenths of the law" most succinctly describes how traffic laws are enforced in Rome.

Pedestrians as Moses

As hard as it is to believe, Rome is a pedestrian-friendly
city, with hashed crosswalks everywhere. Cars, massive tour
buses, motorcycles, and Vespas are all required, by law, to
stop for pedestrians in crosswalks. As a little bitty, single
pedestrian facing mobs of vehicular traffic speeding by, it is
hard to imagine that one has the right of way.

Traffic will not yield to tentative pedestrians, however.
Drivers will only yield to courageous pedestrians willing to
foist themselves into oncoming traffic with a purposeful,
forward look and an I-own-this-road attitude. Incredibly, it
works. Until last week, I couldn't muster this attitude, so I
would wait for savvy Italians to begin crossing and discreetly
follow closely on their heels. I came by some *coraggio*
("courage") this week, and incredibly, when I stepped out
purposefully, not looking right or left, all traffic stopped in
both directions! It seriously felt like the opening of the Red
Sea for Moses. I now look with empathy upon tourists at
crosswalks waiting for the nonexistent green light.

Daily Walk Observations

There is a delicately choreographed dance between Rome's
immigrant street vendors and the Italian *Carabinieri*. As in
NYC, raw capitalism is at work at the über tourist spots and,
like in NYC, the favored products being sold are designer
bag copies and watches. Immigrant vendors utilize an array
of various display contraptions. The moment a *Carabinieri*
comes in sight, the display apparatus and all its goods are
folded up in haste before the vendor then saunters off.
Looking at the faces of the *Carabinieri*, it is obvious they
know what is going on and, within a moment of their

departure, the vendors are back in business. The rapidity with which Roman and New York umbrella vendors appear at the first drop of rain is equally impressive.

There is a defined turf system worked out by the all-too-many beggars who have become fixtures on the streets. Now that I am starting to repeat my routes, I notice the same beggars at exactly the same spots each day. When one is in a new place, things hit one more viscerally. While I see many beggars in NYC, the ones I see here seem to bother me more for some reason.

There is a crippled man who begs on the Ponte Sisto, which I cross practically every day. I gave him one or two euros on my way to class one morning, and when I came back that afternoon, instead of holding out his hat for another handout, he bowed to thank me, as he remembered my modest gesture that morning. And the following morning, he also bowed to thank me. I am more than happy to extend regular acts of charity to him, but many beggars seem less authentically or truly needy, in some inexplicable way.

Rome According to Fr. Diego

A Canadian Jesuit I know who was spending a few weeks in Rome studying Italian introduced me to Fr. Diego, a Spanish Jesuit. Father Diego is an expert on Luis de Molina, a 16th-century Spanish Jesuit Scholastic who, along with a handful of confrères, developed the concept of the time value of money. This Spanish group of theologians is also credited with making the theological argument for allowing interest to be charged on certain types of debt and for developing the field of economics as a distinct area of study.

For the theologically inclined, Luis de Molina is better known for his controversial position in the bitter debate on the respective roles of free will and grace. How do we reconcile an all-knowing God who divinely orders the world with human freedom? Simplifying this theologically complex, yet profoundly important question, let's just say that Molina and his Jesuit confrères placed greater emphasis on man's sphere of action versus the Dominicans, who weighted more heavily the role of grace.

For the financiers among us, Molina and his fellow theologians, comprising the underappreciated School of Salamanca, developed the first modern economic theories in response to entirely new economic problems that arose out of the disintegration of the medieval order and the rise of the globalization of trade. The 16th century was one of extraordinary change — social, theological, economic, and political. The theologians of the School of Salamanca did an impressive job trying to bring moral order to a world that seemed anything but orderly. A bit like today, perhaps?

We speak a lot about the impact globalization is having on our lives today. The 16th century also experienced a powerful wave of globalization in the wake of the great explorers, such as Christopher Columbus and Ferdinand Magellan. Exciting new products and markets opened up in rapid succession, disrupting the tightly controlled, localized economies of the Middle Ages. Financial norms were also disrupted as the capital needs of shipping, and the particular characteristics of the trading of imported goods, required new financial instruments.

For instance, options contracts — a type of derivative that conveys the right, but not the obligation, to buy or sell an asset at an established price by a designated date — were traded amongst shippers and traders of the 16th century. Options are not a modern invention! Mediterranean traders also developed credit contracts similar to today's options, where the seller of the contract agreed to purchase cargo expected to come in on a specific ship, even if that ship carrying the cargo didn't come in on time for the intended purchaser's needs. Embedded in the pricing of these contracts was an interest cost.

But the charging of interest on a loan, commonly known as usury, was banned by the Church. This prohibition is more understandable to our modern ears if we take into account that in the medieval economy, taking out a loan was generally the consequence of tragic necessity, such as bad harvests, sickness, and fire. Under such unanticipated, difficult circumstances, it was considered immoral to charge interest.

Molina and his priestly confrères were confronted with new and increasingly difficult moral dilemmas in the confessional as Catholic shippers and traders began asking whether their trade practices were sinful. Despite being trained in theology and Canon Law, Molina took on the challenge of understanding contemporary economic issues by hanging out on the docks to observe firsthand, and to question directly, those engaged in trade.

Subsequent to his fieldwork, Molina was the first Jesuit to write at length on economics and contract law and he, along with others in the School of Salamanca, developed arguments justifying the charging of interest. In the more capital-intensive economies of the 16th century, loans were increasingly needed for production, rather than consumption. Under these circumstances, interest represents a fair payment for the credit and inflation risk taken on by the lender. It also represents compensation for the opportunity cost of not being able to use the loaned money for other possibilities. In more technical, financial terms, interest charged on a loan represents a fair payment for the time value of money. All things being equal, one prefers to have a good now rather than in the future. A bird in the hand is worth two in the bush. The time value of money expresses in precise quantitative terms how much more you require in the future to make it equally attractive as having something now … precisely one extra bird.

In his published thesis, *De Iustitia et Iure*, my Jesuit friend, Fr. Diego, wonderfully describes how, by better understanding the complexities of lived reality, Molina and his Salamanca School colleagues advanced economic science. Likewise, complexities abound in today's economy. I think it behooves theologians and clergy today to follow Molina's example and 'get dirty' in the trenches before rendering judgment on today's financial, economic, and energy practices.

Where Molina and his confrères got themselves in a bit of hot water and for what they are better known, is in how they applied, or stretched, moral theology to 'fit' complex life circumstances. Theologians refer to this as casuistry, a word derived from the Latin *casus*, meaning "case." In order to avoid falling into this error of revising principles on a case-by-case basis, the challenge is to address all the messy details of lived reality without compromising the principles of Catholic moral theology.

Having lived in Rome for a few years already, Diego kindly let me in on all he had already learned about things Roman. One day, while driving back into Centro Storico after a weekend trip with his mother, the roads around his residence were all blocked to traffic for some inexplicable reason. At the first roadblock that Diego and his mother encountered, the *Carabinieri* insisted he turn around, as did the second *Carabinieri* at another road leading to his destination. At the third obstacle, Fr. Diego having realized following orders would get him nowhere, decided to own the law. He argued in an authoritarian tone of voice: "There was no fair warning ... I am transporting my elderly mother, etc." Suddenly, the *Carabinieri* turned his back to Fr. Diego, initially making him even angrier to be "dissed" in such a fashion, until it dawned on him that it was the *Carabinieri's* way of ceding the law and inviting him to drive right on through. Can you imagine this happening in the United States?

Moving Tourists

Moving tourists around Rome has become a creative art. In addition to the new Segway tours, I've noticed a number of bike tours, which I had never noticed in Rome before. What helped catalyze these bike tours? The establishment of a short-term, urban bike rental system, according to Fr. Diego. I had noticed a couple sets of rental bike racks during my exploratory walks, but they were all empty, and I thought this odd. According to Fr. Diego, Roman entrepreneurs have more or less taken control of these municipality-funded racks using the bikes to give tours. What a fine example of Italian-style (and increasingly U.S.-style) capitalism, private entrepreneurs making a profit off the government.

Old-fashioned walking tours, with umbrella-toting leaders, still abound, though now with personalized audio systems to facilitate listening. And, of course, the double-decker bus tours. I took one of these soon after I arrived to get a sense of Rome's layout, only to abort the ride prematurely when, suddenly, there was a mini-explosion. One of the tires blew.

Recycling Roman Style

Rome has embraced recycling, I think. One of the only points the owner of my apartment emphasized when I arrived was the importance of separating the trash. In the kitchen are four sets of trashcans with different colored bags for each type of trash: paper, organic, non-recyclable, and a mystery category. Based on the directions of my apartment owner, and on the complicated, color-coded recycling direction sheet on the front door of my building, I am still uncertain as to what is considered recyclable.

Making things even more complicated, I can never remember which day I am supposed to put out which type of trash. Each day of the week is designated for a different type of trash pickup. And according to the rules one is supposed to put out the trash between 7:00 a.m. and 8:30 a.m. I often leave after 8:30 a.m. and, given the 73-step altitude of my apartment, I haven't been eager to make special trash trips, so I started to accumulate trash. Until one day I noticed when leaving my apartment at 10:30 a.m., trash bags were still sitting outside all the front doors in the neighborhood. Phew, some added window time there.

To further dispel of the rigidity of Italian law, Fr. Diego dismissively remarked that recycling in Rome is nothing but a charade. All the trash goes to the same place. After all the thought and diligence that I had been exerting properly separating my four categories of trash, I chose not to believe him. Until I actually saw my first trash pickup operation live this past week with the trash guy throwing various color-coded trash bags all into the same truck. I choose to believe that these bags are painstakingly separated at their final destination.

Sad Economics

On a more pessimistic note, I just read a *New York Times* editorial by Frank Bruni, titled "Italy Breaks Your Heart," which rings true to me with respect to the dismal job market and dysfunctional political situation. What he doesn't mention are Italy's scary demographics, which further cloud its future. Italy's current fertility rate is only 1.4, having hovered between 1.2 and 1.4 (replacement rate) since the late 1980s. The U.S. rate has hovered between 1.9 and 2.1 since 1970. Europe's demographic meltdown is a critical issue with profound implications, most of them negative.

The owner of my apartment, a former management consultant, is fairly critical of Italy's political and economic situation and highly recommended that I read a *Corriere della Sera* editorial, published by two political economists who have Harvard and MIT teaching credentials, titled "A Country in Decline Is One That Crowds Out Those Who Are Productive." Instead of dividing Italy up between north and south, the authors draw a line of delineation between Italians who are producing world-class exportable products and those who are thwarting this productive activity through cronyism, excessive bureaucracy, and labor rigidity, and the lack of a well-functioning capital market. I think it is spot on.

It seems that thoughtful folks in Europe and the United States increasingly understand our current challenges and have identified constructive solutions, but our respective political systems have degenerated to a point that renders them incapable of addressing the problems. The question of *why* our political systems have become so dysfunctional is another discussion.

Father Diego says Rome is a city of takers as opposed to producers, with its finances dependent on tourists, government, and the Church. From what I have seen so far, I can't argue with this assessment, though, as a Romanized tourist, I cannot complain.

Roman Tour Guide

"Halloween" Roman Style

This has been a long holiday weekend in Italy. In New York City, the weekend was marked by Halloween celebrations and the wonderful marathon, which I dearly missed. Here in Rome, we have been commemorating all the saints (November 1) and souls (November 2) who preceded us on this earth. Michelle, Worldfund's first employee and now a good friend, visited me these past few days, allowing me to play Roman tour guide for the first time.

On the top of our to-do list was a visit to the Santa Maria della Concezione dei Cappuccini, a church known for its elaborate, if not macabre, decorations incorporating the bones of some 4,000 Capuchin Friars. The Capuchin Friars were established in 1520 as an offshoot of the Franciscan order, which St. Francis of Assisi founded in 1209. The church, located in a fairly swanky neighborhood on Via Veneto, right down the street from the U.S. Embassy, was undergoing a major restoration, so we were only able to explore the half-dozen crypts below the church, which have been converted into a museum.

My two favorite crypts were the "Pelvis bone crypt" and the "Thigh and leg bone crypt." Some find the Catholic Church's tradition of venerating relics curious, if not morbid. For those of us in modern, highly developed economies, where death is not an in-your-face part of daily life, a focus on death can be unsettling. Being within touching distance of so many bones was certainly unsettling for me. But I also found the experience edifying and, yes, life affirming, which I believe was the aim of the crypt bone artisans who worked on the crypts between 1500 and 1870. Nothing like seeing the finish line to prioritize and motivate.

A Visit to Purgatory

One would think a church known for its Piccolo Museo del Purgatorio would be open all day on All Souls Day (November 2). Nope. Church visiting hours were 8:30–11:30 a.m. and again from 4:30–6:30 p.m. We arrived to Sacro Cuore di Gesú — located right around the corner from the beautiful Piazza Cavour in the tony Prati neighborhood — at 4:35 p.m., joining a small group of folks, including a few nuns and priests, waiting for the man with the key to open the door. With zero haste, the key man opened the doors. Upon entering, with my finally attuned tourism antennae, I noticed an Italian man confidently making his way to the front right corner of the church. We followed closely on his heels and, sure enough, he entered a small side room where on a single wall hung about 10 frames, in which were scraps of paper and fabrics sporting burnt-looking handprints or fingerprints.

A booklet of typed stories explained the contents of each of the 10 frames. Frame 5 contained: "A photo of the mark made by the deceased Mrs. Leleux, on the sleeve of her son Joseph's shirt, when she appeared to him on the night of 21 June 1789 at Wodecq, Belgium. The son related that for a period of eleven consecutive nights, he had heard noises, which almost made him sick with fear ..."

According to the booklet explanation of frame 5, the deceased Mrs. Leleux reminded her son of his duty to attend Mass, per his father's will. She also chided him for his dissolute way of life and begged him to repent and do good works for the Church. Joseph took his deceased mother's warnings seriously, converted, and founded a religious congregation before his death in 1825.

By the time we exited, there was a long line of folks waiting to get into this nondescript but extraordinary little room.

Some More Fantastic Church Art

I then took Michelle to see the two Caravaggio paintings I so love in Santa Maria del Popolo. Unlike me, she travels with a smartphone and looked up what else might be of interest in the church. Wouldn't you know? There are two wonderful Bernini statues that I had missed, located near the entrance of the church in the Chigi Chapel: *Habakkuk and the Angel* and *Daniel and the Lion.*

Earlier in the week, I unexpectedly happened upon another Caravaggio located in the beautiful Basilica of Sant'Agostino, slightly north of the Pantheon and Piazza Navona. I had never seen or heard of this minor basilica, which holds the remains of St. Monica, the long-suffering mother of the great St. Augustine.

Upon entering, in the first chapel on the left, hangs Caravaggio's *Madonna dei Pellegrini.* Like all his works, it is a masterpiece of composition, light, color, and realistic detail. While I did not care for how Caravaggio portrayed the Madonna's stance, I was struck by how he painted her right hand grasping at baby Jesus, exactly as Michelangelo did in the Pietà.

Fantastic Private Art Collections

Over the past 10 days, I visited two delightful family-run, private collections — Palazzo Colonna and Palazzo Doria Pamphilj. Both are housed in palaces of prominent, old

Roman families, each boasting their own family pope: Pope Martin V (Colonna; reigned 1417–1431) and Pope Innocent X (Pamphilj; reigned 1644–1655).

The Palazzo Colonna did not have as many major works as the Doria Pamphilj, but the tasteful opulence of the palace was stunning. Of the massive art collection, which covered all the wall space of nearly all the rooms, I was most struck by three large, unusual, and modern-looking paintings by an artist I had never heard of, Ridolfo del Ghirlandaio (Florence, 1483–1561) — *Venere e Amore, La Notte,* and *Aurora.*

What I loved most about my Doria Pamphilj visit was the taped tour, recorded by an adopted descendant of the family, Jonathan Pamphilj. There are a number of Brits who married into the Pamphilj family, which I think may explain the family's more civic-oriented mindset, that of being stewards of a great collection that must be well maintained and made available to the public. Jonathan speaks with a beautiful British accent and recounts personal family stories about growing up in the palazzo, including one in which he and his sister found themselves in big trouble for roller-skating on the beautiful old terrazzo floors of one of the grand salons.

The fantastic Pamphilj collection, which is better organized and better signed than the Palazzo Colonna, includes two Caravaggio's and a stunning Velázquez portrait of Pope Innocent. Those who love the Frick Museum in New York City, would also love the Doria Pamphilj and the Palazzo Colonna. I also plan to visit three additional privately run villa collections: Palazzo Farnese (now the French Embassy), Galleria Borghese (located in the Villa Borghese), and Villa Farnesina, very close to my apartment.

Some Sacred Music

This is a big week on the music front, as I plan to attend a number of concerts that are part of the Twelfth Annual International Festival of Sacred Music. I worked hard securing seats. After careful study of the website, I figured out that one could only secure seating at this series of nine concerts if one is a benefactor of the Sacred Music Foundation, so I made a donation. Success! I subsequently received an email inviting me to pick up a special badge at an office near the Vatican granting me entrance to all the concerts.

I attended my first concert of the series last night, and shall never forget it! Held at the beautiful Basilica di Santa Maria Maggiore, where Pope Francis snuck out to pray the morning after he was named pope, the program included the Moscow Synodal Choir and the Pontifical Sistine Chapel Choir. My three favorite pieces of the evening were sung by the Russian choir and were absolutely beautiful! They were:

Traditional Slavic Christmas song, "*Ot Junosti Mojeja*" ("From My Youth")

Georgy Sviridov (1915–1998), "*Ljubov Svjataja*" ("Sacred Love")

Hilarion Alfeyev (b. 1966, Russian Orthodox Bishop): "*Vo Tzarstvii Tvoem*" ("In Your Kingdom")

Mozzarella, Museums, and Movies

Just as I was starting to slip into that deadened routine zone where, during one's daily activities, thinking crowds out observation, I was thrust again into my role as Roman tour guide. Some New York City friends came to visit for a week, staying in a beautiful and peaceful converted convent hotel, Hotel Donna Camilla Savelli, right around the corner from my own peaceful apartment.

Mozzarella

I tend to eat at restaurants only when invited by new Roman friends, or with visitors, so this afforded me an entire week of nonstop restaurant eating. One of our more memorable meals was at Due Ladroni, recommended by a close friend back home but closed on my first visit. True to its online reviews, the food was fabulous, the service terrific, and the (other) customers beautiful but low key. It is the first Roman restaurant thus far that focuses on fish and does it very well.

Despite the great fish choices, I could not resist one of my all-time favorite food combinations. For my *primo plato*, I ordered a plate of *mozzarella di bufalo* and prosciutto. Fantastic! While I had already enjoyed some of the best-tasting mozzarella I had ever eaten, purchased at a small *salumeria* in Trastevere, I had never tasted prosciutto so tender and flavorful. It is a mystery to me why the rubber balls called mozzarella sold in American supermarkets have the same name as the soft, gooey-inside, a-touch-pungent delight sold here in Italy.

Mozzarella originates in Campania, the region which proudly boasts the city of Naples. The best mozzarella is made from buffalo milk, rather than cow milk, and the first known mention of mozzarella comes from a late 16th-century cookbook. According to the Mozzarella di Bufala trade association, cited in Wikipedia:

> The cheese-maker kneads it with his hands, like a baker making bread, until he obtains a smooth, shiny paste, a strand of which he pulls out and lops off, forming the individual mozzarella. It is then typically formed into ball shapes or in plait. In Italy, a 'rubbery' consistency is generally considered not satisfactory; the cheese is expected to be softer.

Borghese Gallery:
Fantastic Art, Miserably Managed Museum

The four highlights from my New York City friends' stay in Rome were visits to the Borghese Gallery, the Scavi, a guided tour of the Vatican Museum and Sistine Chapel, and a music concert. All required advanced planning and were well worth the effort.

The ground floor of the Borghese Gallery is spectacular from an architectural and sculptural point of view. I have never studied architecture or interior design but, nevertheless, the beauty and harmony of the Baroque-style villa of the Borghese family makes a strong impression on even a neophyte. There is a lot going on, but it all fits together so perfectly. In one main room, the color scheme, embodied in an array of different materials, is made up of golden oranges, pinks, and a touch of green. If someone had told me that pink and orange could look fantastic together, I never would have believed it before seeing the Borghese Gallery. And the sculptures, many of them by Bernini, are otherworldly. The upstairs painting galleries were also interesting, but they were not as arresting as the downstairs.

What made a big, negative impression on my three New York City friends and me was the extraordinarily dysfunctional nature of the check-in process and the rudeness of the staff. Entering and exiting the gallery required five separate lines in one tiny space with a single entry-exit door, minimal signage, and little help from the museum staff.

Having lived in Budapest in the mid-1980s, the Borghese Gallery visit prompted memories of the lines and attitudes I experienced in communist Hungary. It is unconscionable that the experience of viewing such an extraordinary treasure is undermined by such ineptness and indifference. To top it off, the tickets and recorder guide, which explained only a small handful of the paintings, cost $25, which, relative to other Roman sites, is no bargain.

I had assumed the Borghese Gallery was privately owned and managed, like the Galleria Doria Pamphilj and the Palazzo Colonna. Accordingly, I was baffled as to why this most important 'private' gallery was run so poorly. In fact, the Borghese Villa was sold to the Italian government in 1902 and later converted into a public gallery, managed by the government. I write this with a thread of hope that someone who can make a difference may eventually read this.

Scavi and the Bones of St. Peter

In contrast, our Scavi ("excavations") visit represented the height of organization and professionalism. The Roman Catholic Church definitely has something over the Italian government when it comes to moving crowds and making accessible her treasures. Right on the dot at 1:45 p.m., our fantastic Hungarian tour guide greeted us and guided us through the Scavi (tombs) under St. Peter's Basilica. (Here, I am compelled to make a positive observation about a country I also love, Hungary.) There is so much to say about the Scavi, and one truly must experience them to fully appreciate their importance.

A few memorable notes: The present day St. Peter's Basilica (construction began in 1506 and took over 100 years to complete) is the second basilica built on the site. In the fourth century, Emperor Constantine built the first basilica on a hill that served as a burial ground for both pagans and Christians. At the foot of this hill, where St. Peter's Square now stands, was a Roman circus, in the middle of which was erected the large obelisk that still stands today in the square.

St. Peter was crucified upside down in this square in AD 64, possibly looking at the very same obelisk that is there today. Early Christian faithful buried St. Peter's bones in this hill above the circus in a vaguely marked spot so as to protect the sacred bones during an era of brutal persecution under Nero. The main altar of the basilica is located directly above the place where St. Peter's bones, wrapped in a cloth and placed in a simple box, were believed to have been buried. In recent years, scientific discovery has verified this long-held belief regarding the location of the bones.

Pope Pius XII, a man who had a great appreciation for archeology, sanctioned five renowned archaeologists to secretly work under St. Peter's Basilica for 10 years from the late 1930s through World War II. Can you imagine? A secret dig under St. Peter's in the middle of one of the most brutal wars in history! The archaeologists discovered a number of Christian burial spots, but they could not identify the particular bones of St. Peter with any certainty.

In 1953, Italian archaeologist Margherita Guarducci identified the burial box containing St. Peter's bones, which

had been secretly moved in 1942 by a monsignor, igno-
rant of archaeological practices, for safekeeping. In 1968,
Bl. Pope Paul VI announced to the world that, with great
certainty, they had found St. Peter's bones.

Visiting the Scavi evoked similar thoughts as did a tour
I made of the Holy Land some years back. These experiences have made me truly appreciate the corporeality of the
Catholic faith. Ours is not purely an abstract or ethereal
religion. It is rooted in history, human lives, and sacraments
involving physical substances. We can literally and reverently
touch physical articles of our faith such as bones of heroic
witnesses, the saints, and their physical dwellings. One of
the most-venerated places on earth is the Holy Sepulchre,
where Jesus was laid for three days after his crucifixion
almost 2,000 years ago in Jerusalem. One can crouch into
the small space and touch the actual marble top on which
Jesus laid.

Visiting, touching, and venerating tangible relics of
Christianity can inspire more frequent, confident, and
focused prayer.

It has mine. At Mass, during the consecration, I envi-
sion the Cenacle, where the Last Supper took place. While
praying the Rosary, I place myself in the actual spot where
Jesus was born, or baptized, or crucified. This helps to keep
my mind from wondering and opens me up to lights from
the Holy Spirit.

Praying in front of St. Peter's bones under the high altar
of St. Peter's Basilica made me appreciate how reverently
and diligently faithful Christians over millennia have kept
watch over the first Holy Father's precious remains. Their
reverence and deep faith is a powerful model for us today.

Vatican Tour Guide Extraordinaire, Liz Lev

As with the Scavi tour, words do not do justice to our three-
hour tour of the Vatican Museum and Sistine Chapel led

by art historian-"theologian" and tour guide extraordinaire Liz Lev. She makes art and architecture come alive and speak to us as if they were living people. You will have to go on one of her tours to learn why Noah and Jonah were such important prophets and how their importance is conveyed in early Christian artwork and in Michelangelo's very own Sistine Chapel ceiling paintings.

There is more to see in the Vatican collection than can be seen in an entire week, let alone in one day. Liz identifies a few seminal pieces and focuses intensely on their artistic, historic, sociological, and theological significance. I mention one piece here. After quickly shepherding us through the Vatican Museum lobby, which housed an inexplicably awful collection of modern work, Liz started our tour with *Laocoön and His Sons*. This fantastic, seemingly Baroque statue is Hellenistic — sculpted in Greek Asia Minor around 200 BC — and excavated near Rome in 1506. According to Liz, this statue was a critically important inspiration for Michelangelo's Sistine Chapel figures and is one of the most important works in the Vatican collection.

A Concert for East-West Unity

For our last evening, we attended a wonderful concert organized by Robert Moynihan, a veteran Vatican reporter who recently started a foundation to encourage a closer relationship between Eastern Orthodox and Roman Catholic Christians. The orchestra performed a couple of works composed by the same Russian Orthodox bishop, Metropolitan Hilarion Alfeyev, whose pieces I had been impressed by at an earlier concert at the Basilica di Santa Maria Maggiore. Metropolitan Hilarion Alfeyev attended the concert along with a handful of cardinals.

We were happy that our seats were not directly behind the Russian Orthodox bishop, as he was wearing a large white headpiece, a major view blocker. I would love to learn the formal name of this headpiece. I do not think it is called a *mitre*, the elaborate headpiece that the pope and Eastern Orthodox bishops wear during high Masses.

A Gelato and Movie Ending

I recently discovered the best gelato place in Rome — Gelateria del Teatro. I could not find their website, but this review on the Trevor Morrow travel website is one I agree with wholeheartedly: "And while Rome is full of gelato shops (many of which dish out air-filled, uninspired, and overpriced gelato) Stefano's Gelateria del Teatro is a shining, unique, sincere, and refreshing beacon of culinary hope. It's a place where gelato turns into little cups of art, and merely satisfying your sweet tooth turns into a travel experience to remember."

I admit to four visits thus far, my favorite flavor being Sicilian Almond. My tighter-fitting jeans are not happy so I will have to enter a penitential, no-pasta-wine-gelato-mozzarella phase.

One final note: In today's *New York Times*, I read a movie review of *The Great Beauty*, a film set in modern-day Rome. Whereas many of Woody Allen's earlier movies feature New York City as a central character, Rome is the central character in *The Great Beauty*. The opening scene was filmed only blocks from my apartment on the Janiculum Hill, at Fontana dell'Acqua Paola, at which I am looking as I write these words.

My first morning in Rome, waiting for my landlord…

My first night in Rome

The start of my Vespa adventure

Basilica Santo Stefano, Bologna

Me in my favorite Piazza Navona

Heads of Otranto martyrs in the Otranto Basilica

Padre Pio's tomb in San Giovanni Rotondo

Pope at Christmas Mass in St. Peter's Basilica, Rome

Meeting the Pope

The Pontifical University of Saint Thomas (Angelicum)

A street named after my ancestor, St. Capitano
Francesco Zurlo

The Zurlo family in Naples after our pizza dinner

CONGREGAZIONE
DELLE CAUSE DEI SANTI

Il Cardinale Prefetto

Rome, August 23, 2013

Prot. N. 1678-17/08

Dear John M. Zurlo:

I have received your letter of August 6, 2013, regarding your interest in the Cause of Saint Antonio Primaldi and Companions, the recently canonized martyrs of Otranto.

After reviewing the records, the death of Captain Francesco Zurlo in defense of the Faith is documented in the *Positio* for this Cause. He is therefore numbered among the Companions who have been canonized. For additional information, please contact the Archdiocese of Otranto.

I take this opportunity to express my sentiments of esteem in the Lord with every good wish,

Angelo Cardinal Amato, S.D.B.

_____
John M. Zurlo

Letter from Angelo Cardinal Amato,
Prefect of the Congregation for the Causes of Saints,
confirming that Capitano Francisco Zurlo is a saint.

Day Trips and Other Delights

La Scala

I've left Rome twice since my late-September arrival, both times to northern Italy, traveling to Milan and Bologna. I was able to make both trips in a single day, thanks to the 150 billion euros that were invested in 600 miles of special tracks and tunnels from Turin all the way down to Naples to support new speed trains. Twenty-five years ago, when I lived in Bologna as a student, I remember it taking some 3.5 hours to get from there to Rome. Now it only takes just under two hours.

Naples — where I plan to visit after Christmas and where my mother warned me not to try the mozzarella thanks to a distressing November 25, 2013, *Wall Street Journal* article titled, "Naples's Garbage Crisis Piles Up on City Outskirts: Toxic Bonfires Fuel Mounting Concerns About Contaminated Food and Water" — is now only one hour from Rome.

Thanks to the generosity and efforts of the Milanese grandfather of one of Worldfund's Mexican Inter-American Partnership for Education (IAPE) staff (who also drilled me in Italian during an intensive course I took at Dartmouth this past summer), I had a middle orchestra section seat at La Scala a week ago Sunday for the performance of *Aida*. It will go down as one of my most memorable experiences here in Italy.

I hadn't realized how intimate La Scala is, much smaller than the New York Metropolitan Opera. The size of the venue and strength of the singers — a largely Russian and Ukrainian cast, including the fantastic Liudmyla Monastyrska as Aida — made it feel as if the music was pulsing right through me. Always comparing and contrasting, seeing Liudmyla Monastyrska on stage made me realize that one very infrequently sees large sopranos at the Met these days under Peter Gelb, who tends to emphasize acting, dance, and the ascetic elements of opera perhaps a bit more than traditional managers.

I also noticed that La Scala's season had far fewer performances than the Met: just over 100 performances of 10 operas at La Scala compared with 209 performances of 28 operas at the Met. Most, if not all of La Scala's program was from the traditional repertoire, featuring a number of operas from Verdi during his 100th Anniversary year. While not as "out there" as German opera houses, the Met takes more artistic risks than La Scala.

My financial analyst left brain started rearing its head, and I became curious about budgets and funding. Very telling differences. More than one-third of La Scala's 2012 budget of $157 million came from government funding, the rest mostly from ticket sales. Some $6.75 million of government funding was cut this year (to help pay for the debt on the 600 miles of railroad tracks?), which forced a reduction in the number of performances. By contrast, the Met budget in 2012 was $325 million, with a whopping $182 million raised from private donations. Less than 2 percent of the Met's budget is funded by government grants.

A Milanese Way of Celebrating Mass

I had been to Milan twice on brief marketing trips when I was a sell-side analyst. Quite unexpectedly, I walked by the offices of one of the banking firms I visited, located right behind La Scala. Little did I realize fifteen years ago where I was. It was all work and no play back then.

This time around, my focus was on spiritual things. I attended Mass at the Duomo di Milano and discovered that the Catholic Church has an Ambrosian (or Milanese) Rite, which differs from the Roman Rite that most American and European Catholics are used to.

When the priest processed down the main aisle in the purple vestments of Advent, I literally looked at my calendar to see if it was already Advent, which usually starts four Sundays before Christmas (it was only mid-November). Parts of the Mass were said in a different order than the normal Mass that I was used to. I kept thinking that this priest was making a slew of liturgical mistakes. Being at a cathedral, this baffled me, since I thought these priests would have known better.

Every Roman Rite Mass, no matter where you are in the world, uses the same prayers in the same order, so normally there are few surprises (apart from music quality, a mind-boggling political rant masked as a homily, and liturgical dancing thrown in here and there). But, in addition to the Roman Rite, there are over 20 other rites used by Catholics around the world. Each rite has certain variations in liturgical practice. It turns out the Ambrosian Rite celebrates six Sundays of Advent, compared to four Sundays in the Roman Rite. The history behind why the five million or so Catholics in the Milan area celebrate the Ambrosian Rite is beyond me to recount, but Wikipedia provides a very detailed explanation.

The greatest overall impression I came away with from my 10-hour visit to Milan was that, unlike Rome, it was a city going places — productive, full of energy, with lots of construction. I love Rome as a visitor. But Rome is a museum compared to Milan. Milan feels almost Germanic, and, indeed, I was told that the people of Lombardy (which produces one-fifth of Italy's gross domestic product [GDP] and is one of the richest regions in all of Europe) are more like Germans than Roman Italians. If stop-sign behavior is any proof, then I believe it. In front of La Scala there is a four-way, low-traffic intersection with stoplights. Despite there being no cars coming from any direction and the light remaining red forever, no one crossed the street until the light turned green. It reminded me of the German tourists I see in New York City waiting for the green walk light while literally every New Yorker walks right by them, sometimes right in front of a car with the right of way.

Bologna and Mother Teresa

I had not been back to Bologna since my stay there as a student in the late 1980s. I have such fond memories of the city. Normally I find one builds up positive memories such that the reality, when revisited, often falls short. Incredibly, my seven-hour stay in Bologna exceeded my expectations, despite the rain and cold that greeted me. Bologna is an arcaded city, so not a bad place to be in the rain. In the photo section you'll see the only iPad photo I shot that day, of an arcaded section of Via Santo Stefano leading to my old apartment.

Living in Bologna as a student, I regularly walked by the Basilica Santo Stefano complex, part of which dates back to the eighth century. One of my most vivid memories of my year in Bologna was a talk given by Mother Teresa in this very square. I was struck by how adamantly she spoke out against abortion. As hard as this may be to believe, it was the first time I had heard such a heartfelt defense of life. I was able to find a YouTube video of Mother Teresa accepting, in English, some sort of honor bestowed on her in Bologna on September 26, 1987, which clearly was the reason she came to Bologna.

As with Milan, Bologna has a very different feel from Rome, with a very orderly, sophisticated, intellectual, and clean design. And the food! Bologna is the gastronomic capital of Italy. I brought back to Rome a bag of homemade tortellini that I prepared with olive oil and a bit of Romano cheese. Delectable. Bologna is worth a trip just for the homemade tortellini.

Various Tidbits

A dear friend visited me this past weekend on the way back from a business trip to London. Despite two days of pouring rain, with a brief respite when she took the photo of me in Piazza Navona (one of my favorite piazzas), we thoroughly enjoyed ourselves. I had arranged another Vatican Museum tour with the fantastic Liz Lev. I have visited the museum and Sistine Chapel a number of times now, and each time is as powerful as the last.

Three new and unforgettable tastes I experienced this past week were *ricotta al forno al limone*, limoncello made with pistachio, and *sfogliatelle*. I have tried *sfogliatelle* from Arthur Avenue in the Bronx and Little Italy in Boston, but nothing compares to the one I purchased here at a bakery near Campo de' Fiori. I imagine that it will only be better in Naples. I had never before tried *ricotto al forno al limone*, sweetened ricotta with lemon, eaten as a dessert — delectable. In the Campo de' Fiori daily market, a certain vendor sells about ten flavors of limoncello, which he invites the curious to sample. I made a bee line for the pistachio and absolutely loved it.

I was asked to give a talk at the Acton Institute of Rome this past Thursday on the topic of human capital as it relates to the Catholic understanding of the person and to economic development. It gave me an opportunity to read three excellent papal encyclicals on work and the economy

— Leo XIII's *Rerum Novarum* (1891), St. John Paul II's *Laborem Exercens (On Human Work;* 1981), and *Centesimus Annus (On the Hundredth Anniversary of Rerum Novarum;* 1991). They reflect a profound understanding of how the economy works and man's place in the economy.

I wish you all a wonderful Thanksgiving. I certainly have a lot to be thankful for this year.

In Search of Our Family Saint

I set out early Saturday morning for Otranto, where Capitano Francesco Zurlo — an antecedent of our family, according to my father's genealogy work — was martyred on August 14, 1480. Otranto is a walled town on the easternmost tip of the Italian boot heel. One can actually see Albania (though not Russia) from the shore of Otranto. The trip from Rome to Otranto, via Lecce, entailed trains, buses, walking, and many inquiries extended to skeptical Italians who doubted the feasibility of a round trip to Otranto in a New Yorker's time frame.

Via Lecce

Italy's train system has done nothing but impress me. Every train I have taken so far has left exactly on time. I left Rome's Termini station at 8:05 a.m. and arrived in Lecce at just before two in the afternoon, in the pouring rain. My time for exploring this extraordinary city was very limited, so I braved the never-ending downpour and explored the city center as the beautiful limestone streets started flooding.

During a rest break at an empty bar right across from the beautiful Duomo di Lecce, the owner frustratingly explained that we were in the middle of a Neptune storm and that it would continue like this for the next two days. Normally Lecce is packed with both locals and tourists strolling the extraordinarily beautiful streets. This evening I had Lecce virtually to myself.

Some call Lecce the Florence of the south. It is a small Baroque city par excellence, filled with spectacular churches. Whereas Roman churches tend to be undistinguished on the exterior and extraordinary inside, Lecce's churches are gorgeous inside and out. Lecce's aesthetic claim to fame is the sublimely sculpted limestone making up the beautiful Baroque-to-the-hilt facades and altars of Lecce's many churches and public buildings.

One of the paintings that struck me was located at a side chapel of the Basilica di Santa Croce. The painting depicts the vegan, animal-lover saint, Francis of Paola (1416–1507), named after the more famous St. Francis of Assisi. St. Francis of Paola had the gift of prophecy and predicted the Turkish invasion of Otranto. The limestone-carved altar in this side chapel depicts many scenes of his life and prophecies, including the Otranto invasion itself.

The owner of the bed and breakfast I stayed at suggested that I not trust the online Otranto bus schedule. So I returned to the train station, which also serves as a bus station, to check on the times in person. Once there, and after many inquiries, I found a remote office at the end of one of the train track platforms where a very friendly ticket agent shook his head when I asked about Sunday round-trip tickets to Otranto. After some checking he discovered that indeed I could get to Otranto and back in one day via a connection in some town along the way. The total round-trip cost for the 80-kilometer round trip, 7 euros! A deal!

I woke up Sunday morning to an unexpected surprise … sun! My experience with Italian weather predictions is that they are almost always wrong. Like the Italian trains, the bus to Otranto took off right on time. But it did not arrive on time to my connection town, as we were held up for 30 minutes or so for a road race held in the middle of a tiny town called Zollino.

I had always been struck by the number of Italians jogging about New York City in the days and weeks leading up to the New York City Marathon. I had not fully appreciated Italy's running culture until seeing this rather large road race in a tiny town in Italy's boot heel. Thankfully, the connecting bus waited for us, and twenty minutes later I arrived to a deserted train/bus station outside Otranto's walled center.

Otranto's history extends back to BC times, largely because of its strategic location. Only in Spain have I seen the walls of ancient towns in such great shape. However, the great walls were not able to thwart the Turks from overtaking this strategically important town in 1480.

On July 28, 1480, Mehmed II sent Gedik Ahmed Pasha and 18,000 Turkish soldiers to conquer Brindisi, but the winds blew them off course and they landed near Otranto. The hope was to establish a southern foothold for the Turks' European expansion. The 6,000 citizens of Otranto and soldiers of King Alfonso of Aragon, led by Francesco Zurlo, held off the Turks for fifteen days, until August 12, when the Turks were able to break through the city walls.

According to the pamphlet I picked up at the basilica of Otranto, "Captains Francesco Zurlo and Giannantonio Delli Falconi fell heroically while trying to contain the enemy attack." According to my father, Capitano Francesco Zurlo was cut in half at the stomach.

And according to some Internet research:

Francesco Zurlo, Lord of Pietragallo, Oppido, Casalaspro, Atisciano and Brittoli, belonged to the aristocratic branch of the Apulian Piscicelli Neapolitan family who had adopted the name Zurlo, widespread fish in the sea of Otranto, to stand out from the original branch. The chronicle of the family is recorded since ancient times and

has enjoyed, with mixed success, nobility in Naples and in Salento.

I surmise that the "mixed success" is what led my
great-grandfather to come to America. I am proud to say
that we also have our requisite family cardinal, Giuseppe
Maria Capece Zurlo, 1711–1801.

Two days after the Turks killed Zurlo and Falconi, on
August 14, they rounded up 800 men of Otranto over the
age of 15 and ordered them to renounce their Christian faith
and convert to Islam. Led by the tailor, Antonio Primaldo,
they all refused and were beheaded on Colle della Minerva,
now called the Hill of Martyrs. Legend has it that Primaldo
was the first to be beheaded and that his body, though head-
less, remained standing throughout the entire slaughter.

Thirteen months after the slaughter, King Alfonso
retook Otranto, gathered up the 800 bodies, which were
left unburied on the hill, and had 560 of them placed in
the Otranto Basilica (see photo section) and 240 brought
to Naples, where they are now venerated in Chiesa di Santa
Caterina a Formiello. The Otranto Basilica, built in the 11th
century, is also famous for its remarkably preserved floor
mosaic depicting the history of man from the fall of Adam
to the Resurrection.

On October 5, 1980, Pope John Paul II visited Otranto
to celebrate Mass on the 500th anniversary of the martyr-
dom. The 800 were beatified by Pope Clement XIV back in
1771. On July 6, 2007, Pope Benedict XVI issued a decree
stating that they were killed out of "hatred for their faith,"
officially designating them as martyrs. Then, on May 12,
2013, Pope Francis canonized the 800 martyrs of Otranto,
including Francesco Zurlo. It was a touching experience to
spend the day in this beautiful, historic town, which is very
proud of its storied history. One highlight among many was
seeing a street sign with our family name.

I woke up early yesterday morning (Monday) and caught a train north to Foggia. My great-grandfather on the other half of my Italian side was born in Foggia. His name was Comincio di Gioia, derived from the verb *cominciare*, meaning to begin, as he was the first and only boy born after a gaggle of girls. From Foggia, I took a one-hour bus ride east to San Giovanni Rotondo, the remote home of Saint Padre Pio, who lived at San Giovanni Rotondo from 1916 until his death in 1968.

Padre Pio is a saint I was introduced to by three friends from NYC, who are sisters (one named Pia) with a great devotion to the Capuchin Friar. He is well known for telling the faithful to "pray, hope and don't worry." Padre Pio was born into a very humble family east of Naples, led an extraordinarily holy life and, from early youth, was privileged to see visions of his guardian angel, Jesus, and Mary.

Padre Pio suffered greatly throughout his life: from poverty that prevented him from a formal education, ill health requiring him to live at home for several years after his ordination to the priesthood, from the stigmata and, perhaps most painfully, from detractions made largely out of envy for his spiritual fame, which he did not seek. Perhaps it was during this difficult period that he made the comment for which I most appreciate Padre Pio: "It is by means of trials that God binds to Him the souls He loves." I have been consoled by this plainly articulated truth of our faith and have consoled many others by it.

Two other facts about Padre Pio's life made a profound impact on me. He spent hours in the confessional and many people — rich, powerful, and poor alike — flocked to him to have their confessions heard. Padre Pio was not a warm and fuzzy confessor. He was gruff, to the point, and had a gift for reading souls. Ersatz penitents were treated to tough love from Padre Pio. I shudder to think what Padre Pio would have said to the *I'm OK — You're OK* author if given a chance. To keep me honest, I often think of Padre Pio when I enter the confessional.

The other fact that deeply impressed me was the friendship between Padre Pio and Pope St. John Paul II. Their friendship began during a week the future pope spent in San Giovanni in 1947 while he was studying the writings of St. John of the Cross at the Angelicum. In fact, he was so attracted to Carmelite spirituality and its mystics, like San Juan de la Cruz, St. John of the Cross, St. Teresa, and St. Thérèse, that he asked his bishop if he could enter a Carmelite monastery. His bishop denied John Paul II's request because he thought he would be more "useful" as a secular priest. Definitely a lesson in why obedience can bear fruits that are visible even here on earth. While in Rome, he heard of a man that many considered a living mystic, and sought to spend time with the friar at San Giovanni Rotondo. Some believe that Padre Pio, during that first week of getting to know John Paul II, 'warned' him that he would be named pope one day. John Paul II did openly admit later that Padre Pio revealed to him that, of the wounds he bore, (stigmata) of Christ, the shoulder wound caused him the most suffering. This most painful and unknown of Christ's wounds came from carrying the Cross. Knowing this makes me appreciate Simon of Cyrene even more. Like so many of us, when first pressed into service or asked to accept our own cross, Simon was reticent. Indeed, he was "forced" to help Jesus carry the cross. But, I feel certain that after sharing the weight of the Cross with Jesus, he fell in love with him and became his fierce protector.

When I arrived to San Giovanni Rotondo, it was a cold and rainy Monday. What a gift! It meant there was practically no one else around so I had the great pilgrimage site to myself. San Giovanni receives some 8 million pilgrims a year — versus around 5 million for Lourdes and 3 million for Fatima and 12 million for the Basilica of Guadalupe.

I immediately made my way to the original church and attached apartment, where Padre Pio served as a priest. The Blessed Sacrament was exposed and there were a handful of faithful kneeling in Adoration. Kneeling in this great saint's church, where he celebrated Mass with extraordinary reverence and sat hour after hour in the confessional, made me feel very close to Padre Pio. Viewing his simple, personal effects, which were thoughtfully displayed in his simple apartment, made him 'real,' made me think he was a normal person like you and me ... yet not.

Truthfully, I was not overly eager to visit the large, newly erected, modern church designed by Renzo Piano, owing to my preference for classically designed churches. I was surprised and awed, though, when I descended to the tomb chapel below. (Jesuit Marko Rupnik's mosaics covering the walls and vaulted ceiling of the tomb chapel are spectacular.) And then, behind the altar, I saw the partially incorrupt Padre Pio, dressed in his simple brown tunic, lying as if he were peacefully sleeping.

At 5:30 p.m. I boarded a bus to Rome and arrived home at about 11 p.m. to see my street beautifully decorated with Christmas lights! Rome is bursting with Christmas decorations and activity. Italy at Christmastime is very special.

Pope Francis' First Major Solo Communiqué

Pope Francis's *Evangelii Gaudium* (*The Joy of the Gospel*), published last week, has received much attention from Catholics and non-Catholics alike. Traditionally, a new pope's first major communiqué provides a window into how the pope will orient his pontificate. With unprecedented speed, Pope Francis captured the hearts of world, so it is understandable that his words are being so carefully considered. A number of you have asked my opinion of *Evangelii Gaudium*, a daunting task, but here goes.

Evangelii Gaudium is an apostolic exhortation divided into five chapters. An apostolic exhortation is "a papal document that, as the name suggests, exhorts people to implement a particular aspect of the Church's life and teaching." Both papal encyclicals and apostolic constitutions have teaching authority in that they address matters of doctrine and Church law. Reflective of Pope Francis's style, the language is informal. But unlike Pope Francis's relatively brief speaking style, the exhortation is long, 216 pages in English, a bit wordy such that it would have benefited from more editing.

In terms of subject matter, it is pure Francis through and through — a passionate appeal to Catholics to joyfully live their faith and reach out to others by proclaiming God's infinite love for us. I was touched by the power and beauty of many passages. Pope Francis is an evangelizer. I think this is what our world needs right now — an authentic, hopeful messenger able to touch the hearts of many, especially those who are not currently close to the Church.

Pope Francis devotes a long section to specific advice toward priests, including how long a homily should be and how many points it should have (a Jesuitical three). This may be in response to his Latin American experience, where the Catholic Church continues to lose people to Evangelical and Pentecostal sects, which place a great emphasis on the preaching of the Scripture." Pope Francis views his primary function as that of a pastor, and he expects his priests to do so too.

The sections that are getting the most attention are the ones that speak about the poor and, like Mother Teresa, Pope Francis is not referring just to the materially poor but also to the spiritually poor. This opening paragraph describes beautifully what Francis views as one of the great tragedies and challenges in today's world.

> The great danger in today's world, pervaded as it is by consumerism, is the desolation and anguish born of a complacent yet covetous heart, the feverish pursuit of frivolous pleasures, and a blunted conscience. Whenever our interior life becomes caught up in its own interests and concerns, there is no longer room for others, no place for the poor. God's voice is no longer heard, the quiet joy of his love is no longer felt, and the desire to do good fades (*Evangelii Gaudium*, §2).

Pope Francis offers a powerful criticism of two elements of today's global economic system: an undue focus on satisfying unquenchable consumerism and an obsessive focus on profits at the expense of people. He also speaks passionately about those who are unable to participate in the economy due to a lack of skills — a challenge that many economists are trying to address, and understand all too well.

> Human beings are themselves considered consumer goods to be used and then discarded. We have created a "throw away" culture which is now spreading. It is no longer simply about exploitation and oppression, but something new. Exclusion ultimately has to do with what it means to be a part of the society in which we live; those excluded are no longer society's underside or its fringes or its disenfranchised — they are no longer even a part of it. The excluded are not the "exploited" but the outcast, the "leftovers" (*Evangelii Gaudium*, §53).

Many consider Pope Emeritus Benedict to be one of the most intellectually brilliant of all popes. His first encyclical, *Deus Caritas Est* (*God Is Love*) is truly extraordinary for its profound insights and beautiful, precise prose. I had the opportunity to attend a small Mass offered by then-Cardinal Ratzinger in March 2003 and found him to be gentle and humble — attributes that are exceedingly rare in a powerful and brilliant person. I believe that Pope Benedict XVI was greatly misunderstood by the broader world. This misunderstanding, combined with his introverted, intellectual bent, may have limited his ability to evangelize in today's noisy, superficial world.

Pope Francis, by contrast, seems focused more on feelings and emotions and, as such, is resonating among broader audiences. In a world in which people are constantly bombarded with information, words have become cheap. Consequently, lived example has taken on an ever-greater importance. Pope Francis's external simplicity and shows of affection are attractive to many. Pope Francis connects with others on a down-to-earth, heart-to-heart level as a means of communicating the Gospel message, relying less on formal language. During the four times I observed Pope Francis addressing large audiences in St. Peter's Square, he could not help himself from looking up from his prepared script and speaking off the cuff. It was these moments that evoked the most fervent reaction.

Pope Francis's word choice related to two short passages about the economy, unfortunately, has overshadowed *Evangelii Gaudium*'s main message.

> [S]ome people continue to defend trickle-down theories which assume that economic growth, encouraged by a free market, will inevitably succeed in bringing about greater justice and inclusiveness in the world. This opinion, which has never been confirmed by the facts, expresses a crude and naïve trust in the goodness of those wielding economic power ... (*Evangelii Gaudium*, §54).

> While the earnings of a minority are growing exponentially, so too is the gap separating the majority from the prosperity enjoyed by those happy few. This imbalance is the result of ideologies which defend the absolute autonomy of the marketplace and financial speculation. Consequently, they reject the right of states, charged with vigilance for the common good, to exercise any form of control (*Evangelii Gaudium*, §56).

Some have blamed faulty translations from the pope's native Spanish. The translation does obfuscate the underlying meaning a bit, but it does not fully explain a critical treatment of capitalism, particularly relative to a more benign treatment of state power, even in its overarching or corrupt manifestations.

Before trying to explain this difference in emphasis, it is important to note that the political economy question is less important to Pope Francis than individual attitudes, which are at the root of injustices perpetrated against the poor. Pope Francis is not a liberation theologian in a Marxist sense as some would have us believe.

Ever since Pope Leo XIII's momentous encyclical, *Rerum Novarum* (1891), the Church has spoken eloquently about the common good, lauding the benefits of a market economy while at the same time warning against its potential pitfalls as they relate to the wellbeing of the poor and weak. During most of her history, the Church addressed the poor primarily at the individual level, emphasizing the importance of personal and institutional works of charity. In his watershed encyclical, published in response to societal ills caused by the Industrial Revolution and the ensuing rise in atheistic socialism, Pope Leo XIII addressed the structural roots of material poverty and the rights of workers. By articulating the fundamental conditions for justice, *Rerum Novarum* established a public voice of the Church in the economic and political spheres, which continues to this day.

Rerum Novarum, along with St. John Paul II's *Laborem Exercens* (1981) and *Centesimus Annus* (1991), are fairly balanced with respect to the attendant evils that both an unregulated free-market economy and an overarching state can potentially unleash due to their intrinsic natures.

Evangelii Gaudium does not elaborate upon broader society and the common good as much as these earlier three encyclicals, but in its brief diagnosis of the structural causes of poverty, it places greater emphasis on the ill effects of capitalism than on the ill effects of an unfettered or corrupt state. Why is this?

First, and perhaps most obvious, Pope Francis and the largely Italian curia come from an experience of capitalism

that is distorted and better characterized by crony capitalism, which indeed *has* pitted the rich and connected against
the poor and non-connected. How can one truly appreciate
the benefits of capitalism when the context in which one
experiences it brings out mostly the bad stuff and very little
of the good?

Second, those in the United States, steeped in an indi-
vidualistic Protestant ethic, view the world differently than
Latin Americans or European Latins. Volumes have been
written about these cultural differences, which are broad
generalizations clearly. As they inform the economic views
of the pope and the curia, Latins have a greater comfort
level with top-down, paternalistic authority, and they tend
to place greater emphasis on communal ties versus citizens
of the United States, who are more skeptical of centralized,
overarching authority and place greater emphasis on freedom and individual achievement.

Third, Pope Francis and the Roman Curia have a more
theoretical mindset, rather than thinking in practical or
business terms. The weakness business-minded people can
fall into is thinking too narrowly and not considering the
broader implications of their actions beyond the economic
sphere. The weakness theoretical people can fall into is
being blind to what works practically. Nothing like being
responsible for a payroll to fully understand how the economy truly works, at least on the micro level.

While I would have worded a few lines about the economy differently, I appreciate that the pope is not writing
only to the United States but, rather, to the world, and that
he is writing from a distinctly Latin American perspective.
The Catholic Church is concerned about the spiritual lives
of people, with a special focus on the poorest and weakest
among us. The Church's role is not to make economic
policy, and when she has crossed this line, she has gotten
herself in trouble. The pope's role is not to make us feel

self-pleased but to push us to grow in our faith, which often requires being challenged.

Evangelii Gaudium inspired me to start thinking more seriously about some topics that I see being addressed among academics and specialists, but which perhaps deserve broader discussion and civil debate: (1) There are profound differences between political power and economic wealth. Power operates on a zero-sum plane whereas wealth operates on an expansive plane. Does this dynamic encourage those from the political sphere to unwittingly bias economic distribution over economic growth policies? (2) How large is the trade-off between poverty reduction and inequality reduction? (3) What are the different outcomes associated with encouraging solidarity and the common good at the state level, versus the community and individual levels?

Two underappreciated root causes of the growing global wealth gap, which I have thought about at length and addressed in my work and teaching, are family breakdown and the separation of labor from financial capital.

Throughout most of history, physical prowess was enough to earn a living wage. Today intellectual and social attributes are increasingly important to securing meaningful employment, thanks to the technological revolution and globalization experienced over the past few decades. The information economy values brains and 'social capital' over brawn, and, as a result, it excludes many from even participating. The great societal challenge we face is that it is much more difficult to develop brains than it is brawn.

Few would argue with the fact that children raised by richer, more educated parents have an economic advantage over children born to economically disadvantaged parents. Wealthier kids receive greater levels of tangible and intangible investment, whether it be schooling, being read to at home, or music lessons.

What does not receive enough attention is the fact that children raised in intact families, whether rich or poor, receive essential benefits that help them do much better than children raised in single-parent homes. An intact family is the best incubator for forming children who do well in school and who then grow into adults capable of participating, and even flourishing, in today's globalized information economy.

Turning from the family to finance, Karl Marx must be acknowledged for identifying the conflict that often ensues when the means of production (labor, whether white or blue collar) is separated from the owners of capital (share-holders). Until the advent of the modern corporation in 17th and 18th century England, the equity capital required to start or support business activity generally came from the same folks who worked at that business. The laborers and the owners of equity capital tended to be one in the same, or at least they came from the same family or clan. Accordingly, the interests of labor and capital were naturally closely aligned.

The corporate structure facilitates the channeling of large amounts of capital into a single business firm. And the ability for a single business to deploy a lot of capital was critical to the industrial revolution and to the subsequent growth of the American and European economies, which underpinned an extraordinary expansion of personal income over the past two centuries.

The downside to the separation of equity capital ownership from labor is that the profit motive may be pursued in a way that benefits shareholders at the expense of the laborer, reducing labor to a means rather than an end. This was a key theme of *Rerum Novarum*, written during the Industrial Revolution when the imbalance of power between capital and labor resulted in large-scale human exploitation.

The challenge is balancing the interests of capital and labor such that capital is compensated adequately for taking on risk while, at the same time, labor is not exploited. I would argue that this balance is harder to achieve since the democratization of equity ownership through mutual and pension funds, and since the dramatic growth in index funds.

Paradoxically, as equity ownership has become ubiquitous such that laborers are now also capital owners, the owners of publically traded corporations have become increasingly anonymous, which contributes to an "impersonal" economy. It is easier to disregard the wellbeing of those we do not know than it is to ignore the plight of those with whom we have some sort of connection.

Strengthening families and figuring out how to balance the interests of capital and labor in a competitive, globalized economy are complex, difficult challenges. Simplistic, hackneyed screeds against capitalism are unconstructive at best.

I conclude with something Fr. Wojciech Giertych, my professor of moral theology, explained to me this morning. Fr. Giertych is the theologian for the Papal Household, a post that has been held by a Dominican since the Middle Ages. The papal theologian's job description is to provide advice to the pope on theological issues, as well as checking papal texts for theological clarity.

Fr. Giertych interprets the parable of the Prodigal Son as having three, not two sons. We all know about the prodigal, wastefully extravagant son and the Pharisee-like son who resents the father's mercy toward his repentant brother. But Fr. Giertych says there is a third son, the Father's dutiful servant who serves diligently, lovingly, and quietly in the background. The role of the pope is to help guide his flock, comprised of his two imperfect sons, to be more like his third son. *Evangelii Gaudium* has things in it that make both sons uncomfortable, which hopefully means it makes them more like the third son.

The Gospel is full of paradox. I believe one of the great strengths of the Catholic Church, played out through the ages, is her ability to synthesize and speak to the paradoxical nature of our human condition and of God. Pope Francis writes in paragraph 143 of *Evangelii Gaudium*, "Where your synthesis is, there lies your heart". (I might add head too.) Debates and tensions among theologians, priests, and lay faithful often hinge on emphasis, and on the ideal balance between two seemingly incompatible extremes.

Christmas in Rome

Christmas Eve Mass with Pope Francis

I had quite an extraordinary experience last evening — great seats for Christmas Eve Mass with Pope Francis at St. Peter's Basilica. Normally this Mass is celebrated at midnight, but last evening they moved it to 9:30 p.m. I snapped a photo at the end of Mass, as Pope Francis was starting to exit.

I have Fr. Mark Haydu, International Coordinator of the Patrons of the Arts in the Vatican Museums, to thank for the tickets to the Mass. He shepherded my parents, another American couple, and me into the Vatican at 7:30 p.m. to a front section reserved mostly for female religious at the side of the main altar. Father Mark knows the Vatican protocol well and worked what seemed to me miracles, to get us past the many Swiss Guards and security staff. He led us to five seats in the third row. The front row of our section was reserved for last-minute dignitaries, such as the king and queen of Spain, who sat there last year. I was awed and thankful for our great blessing.

When we sat down, the basilica was dimly lit. Then the music began to play, leading up to the proclamation of the birth of Christ. All of a sudden, the lights were lit, creating a powerful audio and visual effect. The liturgy and Pope Francis' vestments were fairly simple as far as St. Peter's fare goes. Mass lasted just under one-and-a-half hours, less time than some Christmas Masses I've attended in the United States.

Below is the English translation of the pope's homily, which he delivered in Italian. He seemed tired, which one can well understand. I couldn't help thinking how relieved Pope Emeritus Benedict (whom Pope Francis paid a special visit to a couple days ago) must have felt, not having to publicly celebrate the Christmas Masses this year.

Pope Francis Christmas 2013 Homily

1. "The people who walked in darkness have seen a great light" (Isa. 9:1).

This prophecy of Isaiah never ceases to touch us, especially when we hear it proclaimed in the liturgy of Christmas night. This is not simply an emotional or sentimental matter. It moves us because it states the deep reality of what we are: a people who walk, and all around us — and within us as well — there is darkness and light. In this night, as the spirit of darkness enfolds the world, there takes place anew the event that always amazes and surprises us: the people who walk see a great light. A light that makes us reflect on this mystery: the mystery of walking and seeing.

Walking. This verb makes us reflect on the course of history, that long journey that is the history of salvation, starting with Abraham, our father in faith, whom the Lord called one day to set out, to go forth from his country toward the land that he would show him. From that time on, our identity as believers has been that of a people making its pilgrim way towards the promised land. This history has always been accompanied by the Lord! He is ever faithful to his covenant and to his promises. Because he is faithful, "God is light, and in him there is no darkness at all" (1 Jn 1:5). Yet on the part of the people, there are times of both light and darkness, fidelity and infidelity, obedience, and rebellion; times of being a pilgrim people and times of being a people adrift.

In our personal history too, there are both bright and dark moments, lights and shadows. If we love God and our brothers and sisters, we walk in the light; but if our heart is closed, if we are dominated by pride, deceit, self-seeking, then darkness falls within us and around us. "Whoever hates his brother — writes the Apostle John — is in the darkness; he walks in the darkness, and does not know the way to go, because the darkness has blinded his eyes" (1 Jn 2:11). A people who walk, but as a pilgrim people who do not want to go astray.

2. On this night, like a burst of brilliant light, there rings out the proclamation of the Apostle: "God's grace has been revealed, and it has made salvation possible for the whole human race" (Titus 2:11).

The grace that was revealed in our world is Jesus, born of the Virgin Mary, true man and true God. He has entered our history; he has shared our journey. He came to free us from darkness and to grant us light. In him was revealed the grace, the mercy, and the tender love of the Father: Jesus is love incarnate. He is not simply a teacher of wisdom, he is not an ideal for which we strive while knowing we are hopelessly distant from it. He is the meaning of life and history, who has pitched his tent in our midst.

3. The shepherds were the first to see this "tent," to receive the news of Jesus' birth. And they were the first because they were among the last, the outcast. And they were the first because they were awake, keeping watch in the night, guarding their flocks. The pilgrim is bound by duty to keep watch, and the shepherds did just that. Together with them, let us pause before the Child, let us pause in silence. Together with them, let us thank the Lord for having given Jesus to us, and with them let us raise from the depths of our hearts the praises of his fidelity: We bless you, Lord God most high, who lowered yourself for our sake. You are immense, and you made yourself small; you are rich and you made yourself poor; you are all-powerful and you made yourself vulnerable.

On this night let us share the joy of the Gospel: God loves us, he so loves us that he gave us his Son to be our brother, to be light in our darkness. To us the Lord repeats: "Do not be afraid!" (Lk 2:10). As the angels said to the shepherds, "Do not be afraid!". And I also repeat to all of you: Do not be afraid! Our Father is patient, he loves us, he gives us Jesus to guide us on the way which leads to the promised land. Jesus is the light who brightens the darkness. He is mercy: our Father always forgives us. He is our peace. Amen.

One element of Pope Francis' homily that set me off on a thinking tangent was his emphasis on the shepherds and their being the first to receive the news of Jesus' birth (after Mary). It made me think of Mary Magdalene and how she, too, was the first to see Jesus after the Resurrection (after the Virgin Mother I believe). Both the shepherds and Mary Magdalene were outcasts of some sort. And both were humble to the core. Pope Francis asks us to thank and praise the Lord for lowering himself to become a vulnerable baby. And yet it can be so difficult for us to lower *ourselves*, to think of ourselves as little children in relationship with the Father.

Roman Catholicism has a very earthy element to it, which was conveyed powerfully when the pope lovingly carried a figurine of Baby Jesus, first to a simple straw-lined cradle in front of the altar at the start of Mass and then, at the end of Mass, to the large Christmas crèche. The theology of the Incarnation was represented beautifully in this simple act.

Upon exiting St. Peter's at about 11:00 p.m., we saw a sea of people in the main square, as the Mass was telecast outside on two large screens. There is another beautiful, life-sized Christmas crèche in the middle of the square, which many people gathered around. Thankfully, it was a lovely evening, as the taxi line was very, very long, with few taxis in sight. We decided to walk to the metro, but it was closed. We then walked to a bus stop, but there were no public buses running. So we walked and walked and walked (kudos to my parents who are in their late 70s!) to Piazza del Popolo, on the other side of the Tiber, where we were able to find a taxi to go the rest of the way to my parents' hotel.

I said a special prayer for you all on this list at Christmas Mass last evening. I wish you a happy New Year.

Holidays and My New Favorite City

Life returned to "normal" this weekend after two weeks of visits from friends and family, and an incredible Rome lead up to Christmas, known in Italy as *Natale*. I hope those reading this are faring well, despite the crazy weather I read about on the East Coast and Midwest. It seems to me that this was a particularly good American winter to miss and, in an effort to be kind, I'll not describe the (insert positive adjective) weather here.

Epiphany, the Real End of the Christmas Season

Tomorrow marks the end of the Christmas season in Italy, the Feast of the Epiphany, also known as the visit of the three kings or Magi. Whereas in the United States, celebrations of major holy days that do not fall on a Sunday sometimes are moved, sadly, to the nearest Sunday, in Italy they hold firm to the actual date. In comparison to the United States, the Feast of the Epiphany is a more appreciated and celebrated feast day in Italy, just as it is in Latin America. Until recently, most Latin American and Italian children received their Christmas gifts on Epiphany rather than Christmas Eve or Christmas Day. It seems to me that Americans take down their Christmas trees earlier and earlier. Last year in Maine, where I normally celebrate Christmas, I saw a number of trees being hauled to the dump on December 26. Not so in Rome, where Christmas decorations are left up at least until Epiphany.

I took the opportunity today to read some of Pope Emeritus Benedict XVI's Epiphany homilies, and think they are among his best. One that I particularly appreciated is his January 6, 2013, homily, one of Benedict's last before his February 11, 2013, abdication announcement:

> These men who set out towards the unknown were, in any event, men with a restless heart. Men driven by a restless quest for God and the salvation of the world. They were filled with expectation, not satisfied with their secure income and their respectable place in society. They were looking for something greater. They were no doubt learned men, quite knowledgeable about the heavens and probably possessed of a fine philosophical formation. But they desired more than simply knowledge about things. They wanted above all else to know what is essential. They wanted to know how we succeed in being human. And therefore they wanted to know if God exists, and where and how he exists. Whether he is concerned about us and how we can encounter him. Nor did they want just to know. They wanted to understand the truth about ourselves and about God and the world. Their outward pilgrimage was an expression of their inward journey, the inner pilgrimage of their hearts. They were men who sought God and were ultimately on the way towards him. They were seekers after God.

My New Favorite City in the World, Naples!

One of the major highlights of my parents' visit this Christmas was our visit to Naples, just over one hour from Rome via speed train. My very first impression, arriving in pouring rain with no one on the gritty streets, was not 100 percent positive, admittedly. Due to the rain, we went straight to the Museo Archeologico Nazionale di Napoli, which houses a fantastic collection of Greek and Roman sculptures, as well as spectacular Pompeii mosaics. In the middle of an otherwise empty ballroom-type space on the second floor is displayed the famous second-century *Farnese Atlas* sculpture, depicting Atlas holding up the celestial spheres (the sky).

The museum was frayed, poorly organized, and poorly signed, with a meager few security guards watching over one of the most important ancient sculpture collections in the world. I could go on with my impressions of dismay. In many ways, it seemed to reflect the decline of parts of the city, and like the city, screams of past glory. For those who do not know Neapolitan history, Naples used to be one of the most important cities in the world strategically, politically, and artistically, saying nothing of its immense wealth. For millennia, starting with the ancient Greeks (if not before), Naples was a coveted second-home destination of the rich and powerful; like the Hamptons but with impeccable taste. Its history, culture, and local dialect are strongly impacted by Greek, Spanish, and French influences.

I won't begin to try to explain why Naples fell off its pedestal — effects of Italian unification, epidemics, and wars — but at moments I felt I could be in Salvador, in the Brazilian state of Bahia, Buenos Aires, in Argentina, or, in the extreme, Havana, Cuba — once fantastically beautiful, alluring cities now ravished by age, neglect, and poverty. My first impression of Naples was definitely "third world."

But then, during the next day, touring Naples in the sun, including upscale neighborhoods overlooking the spectacular Bay of Naples and with crowds of Neapolitans strolling (not scurrying like they do in New York City) the streets, I was reminded of the French and Italian Riviera.

Not all of Naples' past glory has been lost. In terms of topography, there is a great similarity between Naples and Rio de Janeiro. By day two, I was smitten, so much so that I plan to return (perhaps more than once!).

Naples is fascinating, multilayered, earthy, gritty, and beautiful in a not always obvious way, but in a *jolie laide* (beautifully ugly) way, an in-your-face-yet-hidden way. It struck me as the anti-Gnostic city par excellence. It is no accident that the crèche (*presepe* in Italian), first created by Saint Francis of Assisi, was popularized in Naples, starting in the 16th century. 18th-century Bourbon Spanish King Charles III, ruling Naples at the time, had a special fondness for elaborate Nativity scenes, which only increased their popularity in Naples. In virtually every church we visited, we saw a prominently displayed, elaborate *presepe*.

Caravaggio and Discovering the Museo di Capodimonte

During our second day in Naples, we visited what some consider to be the most important works of art in Naples. We began with Caravaggio's *Seven Works of Mercy*. This beautiful, complex, and difficult-to-understand painting is located in a nondescript church-museum in the heart of Naples' Centro Storico. To take it all in, we spent some time sitting on the wooden seats set up near the painting, which is hung in a small hexagonal church called Pio Monte della Misericordia. In a single, modestly-sized painting, Caravaggio was able to concretely and earthily convey the seven Corporal Works of Mercy: feed the hungry, give drink to the thirsty, clothe the naked, shelter the homeless, visit the prisoners, comfort the sick, and bury the dead.

Next we went to one of the most impressive museums I have visited, in league with El Prado and just a step below the Louvre, the Met, or the National Gallery. The Museo di Capodimonte is home to works by Botticelli, Masaccio, Titian, Correggio, Parmigianino, Lotto, Colantonio, Simone Martini, El Greco, Caravaggio, and Bruegel. The collection of religious-inspired paintings fills several floors of the museum and requires several days to fully appreciate. What most impressed me was the extraordinarily high quality of the Italian painters, many Neapolitan, who are relatively unknown. Perhaps due to my overly high expectations, Caravaggio's *Flagellation of Christ,* displayed prominently in the Capodimonte, proved to be one of my least favorite Caravaggio paintings that I have seen in person.

The Importance of Pizza and Family

Neapolitan guidebooks place a lot of emphasis on pizza, "invented" in Naples and, indeed, pizza is an integral part of this city. My parents and I ate our first (fantastic) pizza at a restaurant near the archaeological museum, which was relatively quiet on this rainy holiday evening. The next day, virtually every pizza place we walked by was packed with Neapolitans trying to get in or place an order.

Our second pizza of our trip was particularly special because we ate it at casa Zurlo, the home of second and third cousins, descendant from my great-grandfather. One of our Zurlo relatives, a doctor specializing in internal medicine, insisted with all the passion a Neapolitan can muster that the family ate pizza daily because it was the "perfect" food, containing all four food groups.

Dinner culminated in dance and karaoke-like renditions (with electric piano and words on the video screen) of "O Sole Mio," "Volare," and a third Neapolitan song that I just cannot remember. It became obvious seeing the Neapolitan Zurlos that we are blessed with a no-gray-hair gene. My father's two second cousins, who sat on the couch next to my mom, are each close to 90 years old. It seems that a love of dogs also runs in the family!

The most famous church in Naples is the Naples Cathedral, otherwise known as the Cattedrale di San Gennaro. San Gennaro (also known as St. Januarius) is one of fifty or so patron saints claimed by Naples. For those who grew up in New York City, or watched the original *Godfather*, San Gennaro is the cause for ten days of unmitigated celebration every September in New York's Little Italy. Even today, as the Italian population in this beloved, iconic neighborhood has become diminished, the celebration goes on. I understand some of the newer residences with ancestors hailing from Northern Europe haven't fully embraced the tradition.

But the raucous festivals are not the key to San Gennaro's fame. It is his blood. The Naples Cathedral proudly houses a vial of San Gennaro's blood, which is kept in a vault beneath the altar and is exposed for public veneration three times a year: the Saturday before the first Sunday in May and the following eight days; September 19, the Feast of St. Gennaro and its octave; and December 16. Normally the vial is kept for safe keeping in a local bank vault, whose keys are held by the Mayor of Naples. This tri-annual showing of the vial is met by crowds eager to see whether San Gennaro's dried blood will liquefy. It often does. If the blood fails to liquefy legend has it that disaster will befall Naples.

Despite its importance, the cathedral isn't my favorite church in Naples. That honor goes to the Gesù Nuovo, one of the ugliest old churches I've seen on the outside (leaving aside 1970's architectural monstrosities), but magnificent on the inside. What makes this church so special for me is the tomb of St. Giuseppe Moscati, an Italian single lay medical doctor and professor who lived in the late 19th and early 20th century. Pope Saint John Paul II, who canonized Moscati in 1987, described his sanctity in this way: "In addition to the resources of his acclaimed skill, in caring for the sick he used the warmth of his humanity and the witness of his faith." St. Moscati is a wonderful role model for dedicated single persons.

St. Moscati was beloved by Neapolitans for his indefatigable and loving service to the poor. One can see the love Neapolitans have for their doctor saint by the reverence of the large number of faithful who come to pray in front of his tomb. He was a brilliant man; he delivered a number of technical medical lectures in Italy and throughout Europe and conducted extensive research on diabetes, becoming one of the first Neapolitan doctors to experiment with insulin in treating the disease. He was born into a prominent family, his father being a well-respected judge. He died at only 47 years old, having given most of his possessions away. Tens of thousands came out to show their respects during a funeral procession that wound through the narrow streets of Naples in 1927.

Another church in the old Centro Storico

The neighborhood of Naples for which I have developed a great fondness is near San Paolo Maggiore, a Baroque-style basilica constructed on a 1st-century Roman temple and reconstructed in the late 16th century by the Theatine religious order. On the surface the basilica isn't unique. What makes it special is the tomb and painting of Cardinal Giuseppe Maria Capece Zurlo, the sibling of one of my ancestors and a member of the Theatine order. This discovery happened completely by accident. My father and I are loath to walk by churches without stopping in and kneeling a moment. Walking by the side altar, we happened upon a painting of Cardinal Zurlo and his tomb. My father knew there was a Cardinal in the family from the 18th century, but he had no idea that he was entombed in the heart of Naples.

Ending the Year with Spumante and a Bang

A dear college friend and her family — which includes one of my godchildren — visited over New Year's, after having spent Christmas week in Cortina on a ski vacation. Unfortunately for them, it snowed so much that their ski resort shut down the slopes for a few days, preventing them from getting in much skiing!

Rome did not disappoint, though. We had a wonderful time walking the streets and enjoying fine meals together. Splurging on an upscale restaurant, Antica Pesa, for our New Year's meal provided an important learning experience. Upon ordering prosecco, a fine white wine, to start off the evening, we were summarily informed, in a certain tone of voice, that the restaurant only served spumante, a type of sparkling wine. Renditions of cheesy Martini and Rossi Asti Spumante commercials immediately came to mind. In contrast to our American notion of prosecco being sophisticated and spumante being cheap, sweet, bubbly wine, Italians consider prosecco to be the cheap cousin of spumante.

An unexpected highlight of their visit was watching the New Year's fireworks from my rooftop deck. *Crazy*! The fireworks started well before midnight and went on for nearly an hour and from all angles. We stood in the middle of a 360-degree viewing of random and seemingly unofficial firework displays shot off from all parts of Rome! It was a fantastic start of what I hope will be a joyful, peaceful year for all of you!

Last Excursions

Two More Days in Naples

My Roman sojourn comes to its end in two weeks. Very bittersweet. I am excited to come home and see my friends and family, but, at the same time, I am sad to leave a place and an experience that has been nothing short of fantastic. Inevitably, life has become more routine here, less intense on the senses, so when I find myself getting too comfortable, I hop on Italy's efficient and timely speed trains for a day trip or, in the case of this past weekend, an overnight stay. I could not get enough of Naples during my family visit after Christmas, so I returned. I spent most of my two days walking the streets of this intensely entertaining, unpredictable, beautiful, and scruffy city. I plan to return again Saturday with some friends who will be visiting from Maine.

The spectacular view from Naples's highest point, Castel Sant'Elmo, made me fully appreciate the famous expression *Vedi Napoli e poi muori* ("See Naples, then die"). No one is certain of the origin of this expression, but some people attribute it to Virgil, the ancient Roman poet, while others attribute the phrase to the German writer Johann Wolfgang von Goethe in the late 1780s. The castle is best reached by one of three well-functioning funiculars operating in Naples. Going by taxi takes much longer, as the roads up the hills meander back and forth in switchback fashion. To say that traffic can be a problem is an understatement.

Once I arrived at the end of the funicular line, the signage to the castle was excellent, though it failed to indicate that it was still about a 20-minute upward climb.

The Extraordinary *Cristo Velato*

Michelangelo's *Pieta* has its equal in Naples. In the center of the Museo Cappella Sansevero lays the *Cristo Velato* (Christ Veiled) statue by Giuseppe Sanmartino (1753). I won't even try to describe it beyond using the word "spectacular" and making the claim that alchemy can transform marble into see-through fabric. Surrounding this stunning masterpiece are a number of statues and an extraordinary bas-relief of the *Deposition of Christ*, which hangs over the altar. In this small, beautifully designed chapel sits a perfectly organized group of sculptures that truly takes one's breath away.

The chapel was designed by Raimondo di Sangro (1710–1771), a fascinating character described as a "nobleman, inventor, soldier, writer and scientist." Curiosity, brilliance, money, and prestige supported his pursuit of an array of personal interests, including alchemy, mechanics, sciences, and the arts. Di Sangro was educated by the Jesuits and came from a noble family, which boasted a cardinal and a saint. When he was only a few months old, his mother died, and following her death, his father began to live a wild life. As a result, di Sangro was raised by his grandfather. Like Franz Liszt, di Sangro's father, Antonio, returned to the Catholic faith during his later years. He spent his final years leading a very devout religious life after years of dissolute living.

After the *Veiled Christ,* the statue that di Sangro dedicated to his father, called *Disillusion,* was my favorite. It depicts a man trapped in life-like ropes being freed by an angel. Despite his rich Catholic heritage and education, di Sangro served as the grand master of the Masonic temple in Naples, which lead to his excommunication. The excommunication was lifted after di Sangro wrote a letter to the Holy Father and provided a list of other men in Naples who were involved with the Freemasons. He was a complex figure to say the least.

Pizza Taken Seriously

Pizza really is better in Naples. L'Antica Pizzeria Da Michele is better known thanks to *Eat, Pray, Love* fame, but the famed Pizzeria Gino Sorbillo is where I ended up, and for four euros, I ate one of the best pizzas of my entire life.

I learned from the Cellar Tours website that there are strict rules governing Neapolitan pizza:

- it can only be cooked in wood burning brick ovens
- the crust has to be soft and light, that's why the dough is made the day before it's used, allowing the yeast to rise for at 10/15 hours
- the *pizzaiolo* (pizza maker) must be a real maestro, the dough stretching technique is essential and you need at least 2 or 3 years of apprenticeship to become a *pizzaiolo*
- the pizzerias that make the traditional pizza "*verace*" are members of the Pizza Napoletana Association, which offers a sixty-hour "training course based on the practice and on the skills development for the manipulation of the pizza. For this reason after the theoretical lectures we organize group and individual practical work. The program is intended to give the essential concepts to understand the qualified artisanal work and to learn the Neapolitan technique."

I love how seven of the sixty hours are devoted to "theory."

A Day in Florence

Early one morning, feeling restless, I decided to spend the day in Florence, a city I hadn't seen in nearly twenty years. With

Rome and Naples as my new points of reference, it seemed much more pristine and formal than I had remembered. Florence is a city of superlatives, and it is nearly impossible to write anything original about this extraordinary jewel. A major change since my last visit was the fact that practically every church I entered required paid admission. The churches feel more like museums than sacred spaces. I fully understand why it has come to this, but it saddened me.

A highlight of my day was a visit to Biblioteca Medicea Laurenziana (Laurentian Library), the repository of thousands of manuscripts and early printed books. Michelangelo designed the library. The entryway staircase (a ubiquitous Art History 101 slide) is stunningly beautiful. Also stunning are the stained-glass windows, with unique white backgrounds and beautiful, intricate designs of plants, animals, coats of arms, etc. I had never seen anything like them.

On display was an exhibit of Boccaccio's handwritten books and manuscripts, which I found fascinating for the simple reason that they are the only ancient (if 14th century counts as ancient) books I have seen with words and phrases actually crossed out and rewritten. I had wondered how one could write original pieces or even transcribe works and make no mistakes. Mistakes were made!

Boccaccio was born in Florence, but lived a large chunk of his young adult life in Naples. He was a confrère of Dante and, like Dante, wrote in the Italian vernacular, which was revolutionary at the time. Boccaccio is known for his juicy, realistic dialogue and unforgiving, astute character portrayals. Some believe that Chaucer's *Canterbury Tales*, also written in the vernacular (in his case, Middle English), was influenced by Boccaccio's *Decameron*.

My Florence indulgence was the purchase of a handmade pair of gorgeous Quercioli shoes. I came to Rome with a suitcase full of books, and I shall return to New York City with a suitcase full of shoes.

I finish this dispatch with a fantastic and spot-on quote. Before coming to Rome, a friend of mine gave me the book, *Italian Ways: On and Off the Rails from Milan to Palermo*, by the British author Tim Parks, who has lived in Italy for decades. This is his summation of Italians, as an Anglo-Saxon observer:

> "In every aspect of Italian life, one of the key characteristics to get to grips with is that this is a nation at ease with the distance between ideal and real. They are beyond what we call hypocrisy. Quite simply they do not register the contradiction between rhetoric and behavior. It's an enviable mind-set."

Studying at the
University of an Angel

My Roman sojourn has been extraordinarily special, largely because of two classes I audited at the Angelicum, formally named the Pontificia Università San Tommaso D'Aquino. I do not exaggerate when I say that my normally restless mind did not wander for a single moment during the four hours of class lectures I attended each week.

What is a pontifical university? According to the Holy See (Vatican), pontifical universities are "academic institutes established by, and directly under the authority of the Holy See, composed of three main ecclesiastical faculties (Theology, Philosophy and Canon Law) and at least one other faculty. These academic institutes deal specifically with the Christian revelation and related disciplines, and the Church's mission of spreading the Gospel ..."

Technically, pontifical universities report to Rome. *De facto*, they are fairly independent, like so many elements of the Catholic Church, belying the widely held notion that Rome micromanages the entire Catholic Church.

There are some 65 pontifical universities throughout the world, 19 in Latin America and seven in the United States, including Catholic University of America in Washington, D.C., where I will soon be teaching full time.

Like European and American universities, pontifical universities offer three levels of degrees corresponding to a

bachelor's, master's, and doctorate, and most Catholic bishops (and cardinals) have at least the equivalent of a master's
(STL), if not a doctorate, in sacred theology (STD).

During the election of Pope Francis, some commen-
taries highlighted the small number of Latin American cardinals relative to the number of Latin American Catholics.
One important reason is the fact that fewer Latin American
priests have advanced degrees.

The Angelicum is one of seven principal pontifical
universities located in Rome itself. Most pontifical universities are run by a different religious order of the Catholic
Church, though there may be some nuanced exceptions that
I do not know about. Accordingly, each has a very distinct
personality and theological emphasis.

The roots of the Angelicum stretch back all the way to
1222, when the first Dominicans established their house of
studies in Rome. Aside from St. Dominic himself, the most
prominent member of the order is St. Thomas Aquinas (d.
1274), arguably *the* most brilliant mind of the Catholic
Church (and beyond) of all ages. I felt especially inspired to
send this dispatch since today, January 28, is the feast day
of St. Thomas, referred to as the Angelic Doctor because,
according to Pope Benedict XVI, the title expresses "the
sublimity of his thought and the purity of his life." Now you
know why the university is nicknamed the Angelicum.

Thomas Aquinas's writings are a monumental cornerstone of Catholic theology and important to know if one
wants to deeply understand Christian theology. However,
he is not that easy to read, even after being translated from
the Latin. For mere mortals, Aquinas is not leisurely Saturday night reading.

Aquinas's seminal work, the *Summa Theologica,* was
intended as a guide for theology students. It became the
classic text for Catholic education, of which Aquinas is the
patron saint. But the *Summa,* as it is informally known, is

much more than a text for budding theologians. It presents the clear reasoning behind Catholic theology using a point/counterpoint structure. The *Summa*'s 3,000-plus pages are meticulously ordered into three sections — God (containing the famous five arguments for the existence of God), Man, and Christ — each being further divided into many subdivisions.

Aquinas had the intellectual chops and confidence to use non-Christian sources, such as Aristotle, Averroes, Plato, and Cicero and this got him into a bit of warm water with certain Catholic theologians. Aquinas's *Summa* represents the pinnacle of Scholasticism, an objective, rational theology based on the core teaching that all creatures have a God-given essential nature built into them, independent of human thought, and were created to live in harmonious relationship to each other and to God. Creation is something that can be understood by the human mind because it is rationally ordered by God. The created order reveals itself and provides a window into the workings of the transcendent order. Aquinas would consider relativism, the idea that we all have our 'own truth' — the prevailing belief system reigning in the developed world today — as pure bunkum.

In addition to being brilliant, Aquinas was also a very holy man. Three months before he died, while celebrating Mass, he received a revelation that so affected him that he never wrote another word from that moment on. In response to his secretary's pleas to finish his work, Aquinas replied, "The end of my labors has come. All that I have written appears to be as so much straw after the things that have been revealed to me."

Grace versus Nature

There is friendly rivalry between the Roman pontifical universities, mirroring the (mostly) good-natured rivalry between religious orders. One of the longest standing "rivalries" between religious orders is that between Dominicans and Jesuits. I mention this because I am fascinated by the relationship of grace and nature, a difficult but immensely important issue that has challenged theologians and lay people since the beginning of Christianity. Understanding the relationship of grace and nature is also relevant to an understanding of God's covenant with Israel, so Jewish Talmud scholars grapple with this issue as well. Excommunications have been handed down and wars fought over where the *pura natura* line ends and God's *gratia* begins.

Historically, the Jesuits and Dominicans have held different views on the relative dynamics and workings of grace and nature. Generalizing, I think it is fair to say that the Jesuits, rooted in the views of the controversial 16th-century theologian Luis Molina, place a greater emphasis on human will, as it relates to grace's workings, than the Dominican Thomists, who emphasize more the distinction between human nature (or will) and grace, ceding greater power to grace. Any Thomist worth his weight in straw will tell you that grace perfects nature. Jesuits have been known to accuse Dominican Thomists of being dualists (those who radically separate grace and nature), and Dominicans (and others) have been known to accuse Jesuits of being Pelagians (an early Christian heresy that minimized the role of grace in living Christian morality). Ouch!

Good-Natured Rivalries

Returning to more earthly matters, it is clear that the various Roman pontifical universities vary greatly with respect to their funding and hence, to their physical plants. The two spiffiest pontifical universities I visited were the Gregorian, run by the Jesuits, and Santa Croce, run by Opus Dei. The Angelicum is among the lowliest when it comes to physical plant but, I non-objectively argue, the best when it comes to solid theology, especially Thomist theology.

I chuckled when an Opus Dei priest quipped, in response to my amazement at the Santa Croce facilities relative to the Angelicum, "poor doesn't equate to shabbiness." The reaction of a Jesuit friend while visiting me at the Angelicum was, "I need to work hard fundraising to make sure the Gregorian keeps its lead."

One of my Dominican professors explained to me that the reason the Angelicum physical plant is in a state of benign neglect is because the Dominicans are a decentralized order and don't pay as much attention to one centralized institution. In contrast, the Jesuits are a "military" order, managed from the top down, with the Gregorian enjoying a special place of pride and, consequently, greater resources and attention.

One bragging right other pontifical universities do not have is having educated one of the greatest of all popes, Pope St. John Paul II. He attended the Angelicum right after World War II and wrote his thesis — *The Question of Faith according to St. John of the Cross* — under the renowned Thomist Fr. Réginald Garrigou-Lagrange, O.P. The story that most touched my heart about St. John Paul II's Angelicum tenure was how he used to surreptitiously pick and savor oranges from the trees that filled the garden behind the classrooms surrounding the center courtyard. Having spent a winter in Eastern Europe during the Communist era myself, I remember how dearly rare citrus fruit was cherished.

My favorite "rivalry" comment came from one of my Dominican professors who smilingly asserted, "Since Pope Francis canonized one of Ignatius Loyola's confrères, Peter Faber, last week [in an equivalent canonization, where it only has to be proven that the Blessed has already been venerated for many years], I would next expect him to canonize [16th-century Dominican defender of the Latin American indigenous people] Bartolomé de las Casas!"

This friendly, goodhearted rivalry reflects a bit of human- ity that I love, though, sadly, religious rivalries have also devolved into some pretty ugly stuff in the past and even in our own day.

Many non-American priests I met spoke enviously about the residence where American seminarians and priests live while studying in Rome, nicknamed the NAC (an acronym for the North American College). It is located on Janiculum Hill with fantastic views of Rome and, more importantly, fan- tastic sports facilities, including a top-notch soccer field. This provides the North American seminarians with an "unfair" advantage in the annual Clericus Cup soccer tournament comprised of teams from the various seminaries in Rome, largely delineated by geography. At the time of this writing the North Americans are the current champions.

Thomas Aquinas and the Mystics

I audited two classes at the Angelicum. One was entitled *Christian Faith, Hope, and Charity*, which the registration book described as: "The theological virtues, through which a contact with God is established and developed, are studied according to their presentation in the *Summa* of Theology of Aquinas." It was taught by the brilliant papal theologian, Fr. Wojciech Giertych, O.P. The other was *Spiritual Theol- ogy* — "The invitation to spiritual communion with God as presented in the First Letter of St John. Study of selected texts from the Christian spiritual tradition (e.g., Ignatius of Antioch, *Letter to the Romans*, St. Augustine, *Confessions*) with special emphasis on the following themes: God's saving mercy, prayer, the ascetical life, growth in holiness and con- temporary spirituality" — taught by Fr. Paul Murray, O.P.

I chose these two courses solely because of the pro- fessors. I had the privilege of hearing both of them speak in the United States before coming to Rome: Fr. Giertych lecturing about cultural history at Christendom College and Fr. Murray preaching in lower Manhattan about the necessity of descending low in order to reach God. So I knew ahead of time that they were fantastic lecturers, in addition to being highly renowned and, most importantly, holy men.

Fr. Giertych is a Thomist through and through, which means his approach and delivery is incredibly logical and systematic. I considered this my "physics" class, filled mostly with guys, priests in this case; I was one of the few lay persons in the class. Fr. Giertych can be a bit intimidating, but underneath his stern, Polish demeanor is a deeply holy, teddy-bear of a man with a sharp, dry sense of humor. I cannot thank him enough for acquainting me with one of the world's most profound thinkers.

Fr. Giertych's apartment is very close to the papal apartment, which is now empty owing to Pope Francis's decision to live in a nearby residence. Visiting Fr. Giertych gave me an appreciation for why Pope Francis made this decision: Living in the apostolic palace is like living in a museum-like prison, with long, dark corridors, decorated with luscious Michelangelo and Rafael frescos, protected by many layers of Swiss Guard security. On the walls of a long hallway inside Fr. Giertych's apartment are paintings of all the papal theologians going back many centuries.

I arrived to my first Tuesday morning class with Fr. Giertych a tad nervous, not at all sure what to expect. The lecture hall was a bit worn, with a number of broken seats and a tattered curtain doing its best to shield us from the bright Roman light. American seminarians living at the NAC made up at least half the class, seminarians from Europe, Australia, Asia, and Africa perhaps another 30 percent or so, and the rest a mixed crew of nuns and lay folks. Fr. Giertych has quite a following at the NAC and this pleases me to no end because it means America's best and brightest seminarians are being formed by one of the best and brightest (and, dare I say, orthodox) theologians of the Church.

Right at 10:30 a.m. on the dot Fr. Giertych entered the room donning his white Dominican habit, determinedly placed his lecture notes on the podium, and led us in a recitation of the Our Father, the Hail Mary, and an invocation to St. Thomas Aquinas. Depending on the feast day, other saints would be invoked throughout the semester. And without further ado, he started his lecture. No introduction, no 'let me explain how this course works' prelude, just right to the material. Father Giertych spoke with a hard-to-place accent and had me mesmerized from his first sentence. I scribbled notes as fast as I could and, admittedly, wrote out more than a few theological terms phonetically owing to my lack of formal theological training and abysmal spelling skills.

Father Murray's class met the next day, Wednesday, in the same tired lecture hall as Fr. Giertych's class. I felt more at ease entering class on day two. Whereas Fr. Giertych was habitually early, or right on time, Fr. Murray conveyed a slightly more relaxed attitude towards punctuality. He entered class on that first day, like most days, with a shy, endearing smile carrying a pile of books which he set on the table before reciting a prayer. He gave a bit of an introduction and opened the way for questions. Fr. Murray's class was a bit more accessible, though no less profound, and was comprised of many more lay persons and nuns.

Father Murray is a poet and has a melodious, Irish-accented voice (accessible to all through the audio version of his fantastic book *Aquinas at Prayer*). Though Dominican, he has a profound understanding and sensitivity to Carmelite spirituality (as does Fr. Giertych). He has written many books on prayer and contemplation, in addition to books of poetry. He also served as a periodic spiritual director for St. Teresa of Calcutta. This is not something I learned from Fr. Murray himself but picked up from chitchat among admiring students under the Angelicum arcades framing the center courtyard.

Fr. Murray opened our first class by defining spiritual theology. In centuries past, spiritual theology used to be referred to as the study of the ascetical or mystical life, and it tended to be more tightly integrated with moral and speculative theology. According to Hans Urs von Balthasar, whom Fr. Murray quoted in class, "[this] separation of theology and spirituality is the greatest crisis that has hit our Church."

Fr. Murray went on during our first class to explain that spiritual theology is the bringing together of the experience of the divine with reasoned reflection. Piety and thinking are *both* needed. He also cautioned that today experience is too often interpreted as feeling over thinking and this is not a fully correct way of thinking about experience, especially as it relates to prayer.

While we do not all have to be theologians, we should be thinking about our faith like Mary, who "kept all these things, pondering them in her heart" (Luke 2:19). Quoting Blessed Cardinal Newman, Fr. Murray also told us that "St. Mary is our pattern of Faith, both in the reception and in the study of Divine Truth."

A few of the questions that Fr. Murray tantalizingly suggested we would tackle during the semester were: What is Christian prayer? What constitutes the Christian experience, including sin and failure? Is asceticism about hating oneself or the world? Why is the relationship between one's personal spiritual life and ecclesial life so fundamental?

As the semester unfolded we spent a fair amount of time on St. Teresa of Ávila, St. John of the Cross, St. Thérèse de Lisieux, St. Augustine, Catherine of Siena, and Bernard de Clairvaux — all major, contemplative saints and Doctors of the Church.

Father Murray spent the most time on St. Augustine. For anyone who has not yet read St. Augustine's *Confessions*, I say run out now and get a hold of the book. Though Augustine lived in the fourth and fifth centuries, his self-reflections are extraordinarily relevant today. He was the contemplative par excellence, and one of the many lines of his that I love is, "Who am I? I am an enigma to myself. You, alone, Lord, know who I am." St. Augustine spent his early life obsessively searching for the truth, and once he found truth, he obsessively worked on understanding himself in relationship to God. Parts of the *Confessions* read almost like a Woody Allen dialogue.

I was an avid rock music fan in ages past, and will admit to revering a few rock stars as a youngster. Fr. Giertych and Fr. Murray have supplanted and superseded the likes of Mick Jagger, Bono, and Bob Dylan in my heretofore pantheon of adoringly admired living persons. Fr. Giertych can explain the most esoteric of theological concepts, or describe the most complex historical event, in the clearest, most succinct, and simple yet profound way, of anyone I've met. He is a walking grab bag of one- and two-line zingers. In contrast, Fr. Murray has an intellectual, visceral, and supernatural understanding of suffering, struggling, seeking souls like no one I've met. For Fr. Murray, "What happens in this drama of the spiritual life?" is the question that has most urgently captured his attention. It has also led him to a life of adventures and spiritual friendships that are worthy of a motion picture.

On this high note, I approach the end of my sojourn in Rome. I return to crazy-cold New York City this Friday, excited to come home and see friends and family but also saddened that something so wonderful is coming to an end. I can't begin to voice my appreciation for this opportunity, which has given me much-needed rest from many, many years of tireless work and travel, an opportunity to experience intense beauty, learn more about the profoundly rich Catholic faith, meet extraordinary people, create a collection of memories that will last a lifetime, and enjoy the best food and wine in the world!

A Final Arrivederci

The last thirty hours of my Roman sabbatical were among the most memorable, so I am writing a last dispatch. On Thursday morning, Fr. Mark Haydu, the same priest who arranged the tickets for our Christmas Eve Mass with Pope Francis, celebrated a private Mass for me at the tomb of St. Peter, located directly beneath the main altar of St. Peter's Basilica. It was one of the most memorable Masses I have ever experienced and one of the top highlights of my Roman stay.

I met Fr. Mark a few minutes before seven in the morning at a side gate leading to the area behind St. Peter's Basilica. We entered the basilica through a private entrance, along with nearly two dozen other priests also there to celebrate private Masses in the various tombs of the crypt of St. Peter's, where many popes are buried. The priests moved hastily. I later learned it was "first come, first served" in terms of which papal tomb a priest was given permission to celebrate Mass. Fr. Mark quickly ushered me into a very large sacristy, where the priests put on their Mass vestments and collect the sacred vessels used to celebrate Mass.

I had never been in a sacristy while a priest was preparing for Mass. To see dozens of priests in this setting expertly and rapidly getting ready was extraordinary. I was touched that the only painting in the sacristy was one depicting St. John Vianney (the Curé d'Ars), a holy, simple 18th-century French country priest who is the patron saint of parish priests. St. John Vianney did so poorly in his studies, especially Latin, that he was nearly denied priestly ordination. This is the saint whose image is prominently displayed in one of the most exalted places on earth and among the Church's most-learned and sophisticated priests about to celebrate Mass. What a beautiful message of humility.

That night I was awakened by a powerful thunderstorm and heavy rain. It rained a fair amount during my stay in Rome, so I did not think much about it until my landlord, who came to bid me goodbye Friday morning, could not reach any taxi company by phone to order me a taxi to the airport. It reminded me of New York City rush hour in the rain, when finding taxis is nearly impossible. After many tries to established taxi companies, he called Rocco, a man in the Trastevere neighborhood who once drove him somewhere years ago. My landlord rang Rocco, woke him up, and pleaded with him to take me to the airport.

After a 30-minute wait in the doorway of my apartment building, under pouring rain, Rocco came to the rescue. Rather calmly, he informed me that Rome was flooded, the highway to the airport was closed, and the train tracks between the city center and the airport were flooded — but not to worry because he knew back roads to the airport. Nearly two hours later, we finally arrived after being turned back at many junctures by police-blocked flooded roads. We saw walls crumbled into streets, overflowing rivers, and fields that had become mini lakes. I arrived with not a minute to spare, one of the last to board a partially empty plane right before takeoff, as many others never made it. I truly believe Rocco (rock, *Cephas*, Peter) was a miracle sent by St. Peter himself.

With thanks to St. Peter, I say a final *arrivederci* to Rome (for now),

Luanne

Afterword

"I am a daughter of the Church"

I came to love the Church during my four-month sabbatical in Rome. Not that I had ever disliked it. Rather, I took it for granted and was more likely to think of its innumerable flaws — that is to say her flawed members — than her supernatural attributes. "In the end, I am a daughter of the Church" were among St. Teresa of Avila's last words, uttered while she herself was under the disconcerting shadow of the Inquisition. Despite countless and enervating challenges waged by ecclesial authorities and fellow religious against her reform efforts, Teresa never wavered in expressing great love and loyalty to the Church. For Teresa, union with God was inconceivable away from wholehearted membership in the Mystical Body of Christ.

How easy it is to be jaded by the foibles and, at times, crimes committed by members of Christ's beloved Church. Today's leadership and institutions enjoy precious little credibility. This goes for the Catholic Church as well. Love for the Church is inspired not primarily by its good works but by the fact that Jesus Christ created it to shepherd us to heaven, our eternal home. The Church is Christ's great gift to mankind. He loves the Church so much that he is espoused to it. Do we love our family members any less when they err?

Living a short walk from St. Peter's Basilica, basking in masterpieces of religious art as ubiquitous as wallpaper in the 1970's, learning the extraordinary truths of our faith from some of the brightest minds and spiritual athletes of the Church, and enough unadulterated solitude to let it all sink in, fed my appreciation for the miracle that is the Catholic Church — despite the great challenges confronting her at this moment.

I've kept in close touch with most of the people I came to know well in Rome, including Fr. Mark Haydu. Rome is less known for its music than its visual arts. One exception is the Sistine Chapel Choir, affectionately known as the Pope's Choir, under the direction of the exacting Msgr. Palombella. His first name is Massimo, a superlative I suspect Msgr. Palombella deems quite fitting. The Sistine Chapel Choir was formally founded by Pope Gregory the Great in the 6th century and rejuvenated by Pope Sixtus IV. The choir's primary mission is to sing at the liturgical celebrations of the Supreme Pontiff.

Thanks to the tireless efforts of Fr. Mark, the Pope's Choir performed in New York City in September 2017. Given my experience organizing events in New York City on behalf of Worldfund, Fr. Mark asked if I might help him pull off this historic event. The last time the Choir performed in the United States was in 1986. It gave me pleasure to be able to reciprocate Fr. Mark's exceedingly generous hospitality while I was in Rome. The Choir, made up of over 50 boys and men, sang angelically to a packed St. Patrick's Cathedral. New York City exuberantly welcomed the angelic singers, and the singers were enchanted by their time in the city. Thanks to the heightened quality of the Sistine Chapel Choir under Msgr. Palombella's direction, Deutsche Grammophon has recorded three fantastic CDs of the choir, making their angelic voices available to all.

My work since returning from Rome has been more directly connected to the Church. I had taught a graduate course at The Catholic University of America (CUA) on an adjunct basis for a couple years before leaving for Rome. Like the Angelicum in Rome, CUA is a pontifical university, and as with the Angelicum, CUA is governed under the authority of the Holy See and is licensed to grant ecclesiastical degrees in philosophy, theology, and Canon Law. After my return, I began teaching at CUA full time, with courses in finance and a course on education in developing countries.

CUA is located in a decidedly Catholic, gentrifying neighborhood in Northeast D.C. The Basilica of the National Shrine of the Immaculate Conception, which originally was part of the university, is conveniently located in the center of campus. CUA is the only university which has received the last three popes during their visits to the United States: John Paul II, Benedict XVI, and Francis. As a CUA professor, I was given a ticket to the Mass of Canonization for Bl. Junipero Serra, celebrated by Pope Francis at the basilica. Given the opportunities I had to see the Pope in Rome, I gave my ticket to a Mexican nun who had never seen the Pope in person.

During the fall after my return from Rome, two German Cardinals gave major addresses at CUA — Cardinal Müller, then Prefect of the Congregation for the Doctrine of the Faith, and Cardinal Kasper. Despite being quite tall and strongly built, Cardinal Müller reminded me of the diminutive Pope Benedict. He conveyed both brilliance and holiness, a rare combination.

A number of religious orders are located within a stone's throw from campus, including the Dominican House of Studies. Thanks to scheduling acumen, I audited a couple more theology courses taught by Dominicans residing on this side of the Atlantic. One course dealt with the seven capital sins and the other was on modern theology. My inspiration for taking the modern theology seminar was rooted in my compulsion to understand how so many German theologians veered off the road, so to speak. A fruit of the course was a greater understanding of the off ramps plaguing modern theology, though I do not yet have the expertise to explain them succinctly.

My Rome experience has influenced my work at CUA in a couple tangible ways. I took a cue from Fr. Giertych and Fr. Murray by starting each of my finance classes with an *Our Father*. Apart from the supernatural benefit of making contact with God, starting class with a prayer quickly settles everyone down, bringing the class to a calm, quiet, focused state. Well over 90 percent of the students in my classes are Catholic, but I also have a number of Muslim students, largely from Saudi Arabia. I had sometimes questioned myself about whether praying at the start of class might make them feel uncomfortable; that is until Mohammed, one of my advanced international corporate finance students, thanked me after class one day for starting out with a prayer. While we all recited the Our Father, Mohammed used to pray to Allah and was pleased to have the chance to do so before class commenced. I happily discovered that the students appreciated calling upon God and various saints before delving into the temporal challenges of capital structure analysis. And, from a purely practical perspective, there is no easier, quicker way to calm down a class at its opening.

While in Rome I was asked to manage the development of an online course on Catholic Social Doctrine in coordination with the Centesimus Annus Pro Pontifice Foundation. Thanks to a number of conversations as well as thoughtful study of the relevant papal encyclicals, I got up to speed on Catholic Social Doctrine while in Rome and was able to hit the ground running once I arrived back at CUA.

Catholic Social Doctrine (CSD) is something most Catholics have heard about but very few can explain. In a nutshell, CSD provides a theological, philosophical, socio-logical, and economical framework for structuring a just society and for interacting with others, particularly the poor and weak among us.

Loving the poor has been a cornerstone of the Cath-olic Church since her very foundation. While "preferential option for the poor" is a relatively recent term that became popular in the late 20th century, the Church has lived out her mission to serve the poor from her earliest days. Today, the Catholic Church is the largest provider of social services in the world.

During most of her history, the Church focused upon material poverty, primarily at the individual level, emphasiz-ing the importance of personal and institutional works of charity. Since Pope Leo XIII's 1891 watershed Encyclical, *Rerum Novarum*, written in response to a series of political, economic and philosophical challenges, the Church has taken a broader approach to poverty. The Church gathers together and articulates her wisdom about the practical implications of the belief that we are all members of one family and, as such, we have obligations to one another.

This eight-week, moderated online CSD course is open to anyone interested and is offered four times a year. The course can be accessed here: https://business.catholic.edu/academics/certificate/csd-certificate/index.html

Thanks to my work on this course I was given the privileged opportunity to meet the pope in Rome. The Centesimus Annus Foundation hosted a conference on alle-viating poverty in May 2016 during which I moderated a panel discussion. Participants in the conference were invited to a meeting with the pope behind Vatican walls in the grand Clementine Hall in the Apostolic Palace. I assumed that it would be a general greeting as there were a few hundred of us. Incredibly, Pope Francis met each of us individually, one after another as we lined up in front of him. I've heard from others privileged to personally meet the pope that the mind has a tendency to draw a big blank at the penultimate moment of this grand opportunity. While waiting my turn, I practiced something I wanted to say to him in the best Argentine (Spanish) I could muster. I cannot remember if he graciously responded in Italian or Spanish.

Rome impacted me on a more personal level by providing quiet time that allowed me to discern more broadly God's will for me. It was while I was in Rome that I came to realize that God was calling me to Himself as a dedicated single.

The dedicated single vocation is a hidden, little-understood, if not devalued, vocation, not only by broader society, but also by many Catholics, including priests and religious. Indeed, I would guess that most people feel a bit sorry for single, faithful Catholics, even those called to this unique vocation. For many, it is not a vocation that was planned for or dreamed of. Many discern that Jesus Christ called them to himself later in life, often after disappointments.

As a Catholic who has discerned that God had been calling me quietly, but persistently, to be His own as a single lay person, I haven't come across much that spoke positively and directly to this vocation. This, despite the fact that Holy Scriptures and Church history are filled with examples of holy and heroic single lay people who dedicated themselves exclusively to God.

I know of untold numbers of Catholic singles who feel bereft, directionless, unwelcome, misunderstood, and, even, scorned. Pope Francis speaks often about the need to reach out to the peripheries. There may be no existential periphery greater than that inhabited by many single Catholics. More attention needs to be paid to those who God is raising up amidst the rubble of our post-Christian, troubled world: holy, creative men and women who love the Church and are receptive to His call to serve Him exclusively in the world — God's "free agents" if I may call it so.

Due to the need I see out there — and thanks to many who have encouraged me in this effort, including the two Dominican professors I studied under in Rome — I am working on a book about the dedicated single vocation, which I hope will be published soon.

Bibliography

Augustine, *Confessions* X.xxxiii.50.

Akin, Jimmy. "Pope Francis' new document, *Evangelii Gaudium*, 9 things to know and share," *National Catholic Register*, Nov. 26, 2013, http://www.ncregister.com/blog/jimmy-akin/pope-francis-new-document-evangelii-gaudium-9-things-to-know-and-share.

Benedict XVI, Homily on the Solemnity of the Epiphany of the Lord, Jan. 6, 2013, http://w2.vatican.va/content/benedict-xvi/en/homilies/2013/documents/hf_ben-xvi_hom_20130106_epifania.html.

Bruni, Frank. "Italy Breaks Your Heart," *New York Times*, Oct. 26, 2013, http://www.nytimes.com/2013/10/27/opinion/sunday/bruni-italy-breaks-your-heart.html.

Dargis, Manohla. "The Glory of Rome, the Sweetness of Life," *New York Times*, Nov. 14, 2013, http://www.nytimes.com/2013/11/15/movies/the-great-beauty-starring-toni-servillo.html.

Francis I, *Evangelii Gaudium* (*The Joy of the Gospel*), https://w2.vatican.va/content/francesco/en/apost_exhortations/documents/papa-francesco_esortazione-ap_20131124_evangelii-gaudium.html.

— General Audience, Oct. 2, 2013, https://w2.vatican. va/content/francesco/en/audiences/2013/documents/papa-francesco_20131002_udienza-generale. html.

Lapide, Pinchas. *Three Popes and the Jews,* Hawthorn, 1967.

Mesco, Manuela. "Naples's Garbage Crisis Piles Up on City Outskirts," *Wall Street Journal,* Nov. 25, 2013, https://www.wsj.com/articles/naples8217s-garbage-crisis-piles-up-on-city-outskirts-1385340685.

Miller, Michael J. "Joseph Moscati: Saint, doctor, and miracle-worker," Catholic Education Resource Center, https://www.catholiceducation.org/en/faith-and-character/faith-and-character/joseph-moscati-saint-doctor-and-miracle-worker.html.

Morrow, Trevor. "Rome's Fresh and Natural Gelato," Trevor Morrow Travel, May 8, 2013, http://trevormorrowtravel.com/gelateria-del-teatro/.

Mozzarella di Bufala Campana (http://www.mozzarelladibufala.org/allestimento.htm).

Parks, Tim. *Italian Ways: On and Off the Rails from Milan to Palermo,* New York: W.W. Norton & Co., 2013.

Priestblock 25487: A Memoir of Dachau, Bethesda, MD: Zaccheus Press, 2007.

"St. Januarius," Catholic Encyclopedia, New Advent, http://www.newadvent.org/cathen/08295a.htm.

Join the
Association of Marian Helpers,
headquartered at the National Shrine of The Divine Mercy,
and share in special blessings!

An invitation from
Fr. Joseph, MIC, the director

**Marian Helpers is an Association of
Christian faithful of the Congregation
of Marian Fathers of the Immaculate
Conception.** By becoming a member,
you share in the spiritual benefits
of the daily Masses, prayers,
and good works of the Marian
priests and brothers.

This is a special offer of grace
given to you by the Church
through the Marians. Please
consider this opportunity to share in these blessings, along with others
whom you would wish to join into this spiritual communion.

**The Marian Fathers of the Immaculate Conception of the Blessed
Virgin Mary is a religious congregation of nearly 500 priests and
brothers around the world.**

Call 1-800-462-7426 or visit marian.org

Give a Consoling Gift: *Prayer*

Enroll your loved ones in the Association of Marian Helpers, and they will participate in the graces from the daily Masses, prayers, good works, and merits of the Marian priests and brothers around the world.

Enrollments can be offered for the living or deceased. We offer a variety of enrollment cards: wedding, anniversary, First Holy Communion, birthday, get well, and more.

1-800-462-7426 • marian.org/enrollments

Request a Mass
to be offered by the Marian Fathers for your loved one

Individual Masses
(for the living or deceased)

Gregorian Masses (30 days of consecutive Masses for the deceased)

1-800-462-7426 • marian.org/mass

Visit the National Shrine of The Divine Mercy in Stockbridge, Massachusetts!

The Shrine is a ministry of the Marian Fathers of the Immaculate Conception and offers daily Masses, Confessions, prayers, and more.

For more information, visit TheDivineMercy.org/shrine or call (413) 298-3931.

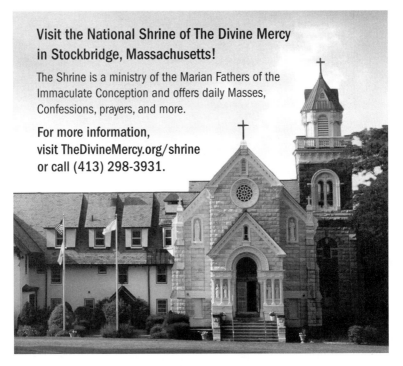